22.92

D0559196

PROUD

THE STORY OF JAMES BROWN

James Brown walks on stage at Shrine Auditorium in Los Angeles in 1969, wearing his trademark cape.

PROUD

THE STORY OF JAMES BROWN

Ronald D. Lankford Jr.

MORGAN
REYNOLDS
PUBLISHING

St. John the Baptist Parish Library
2920 New Hwy. 51
LaPlace, LA 70068

James Brown in London, 1985

TO ELIZABETH C. S. LANKFORD

Proud: The Story of James Brown
Copyright © 2013 by Morgan Reynolds Publishing

All rights reserved
This book, or parts therof, may not be reproduced
in any form except by written consent of the publisher.
For more information write:
Morgan Reynolds Publishing, Inc.
620 South Elm Street, Suite 387
Greensboro, NC 27406 USA

Library of Congress Cataloging-in-Publication Data

Lankford, Ronald D., 1962-
  Proud : the story of James Brown / by Ronald D. Lankford Jr.
     p. cm. -- (Modern music masters)
  ISBN 978-1-59935-374-6 -- ISBN 978-1-59935-375-3 (e-book) 1.
Brown,
James, 1933-2006. 2. Soul musicians--United States--Biography. I. Title.
  ML420.B818L36 2014
  782.421644092--dc23
  [B]
                              2012035353

PRINTED IN THE UNITED STATES OF AMERICA
First Edition

Book cover and interior designed by:
Ed Morgan, navyblue design studio
Greensboro, NC

Brown in 1966

CONTENTS

An undated photo of James Brown as a child

Chapter One

A POOR BOY FROM GEORGIA

When James Brown walked onto the stage at the Apollo Theater on October 24, 1962, his future as an entertainer was on the line. During a series of shows that day, the soul singer would record a live album, and everything—his dancing and singing, the performance of his backing band and singers, and the reaction of the audience—had to be perfect.

Nearly everyone around Brown believed it was a bad idea to record a live album. Bands just didn't record live albums back then. Opposition, however, only made him more determined. Even his record label rejected the idea, believing that there was no commercial potential in a live album with no new songs. Still, Brown refused to give up the idea. If his record label declined to support a live album, there was only one thing to do: pay for it himself. Brown used $5,700 of his own money, a large sum in 1962, and started making arrangements.

When Brown walked out on the stage of the Apollo Theater, the premier music spot for black entertainers during the 1960s, he knew that his reputation was at stake. Failure was not an option. He screamed. Sweated. And slipped and slid across the stage, dropping down hard to his knees and to splits.

Brown's intuition turned out to be right. The recording, *Live at the Apollo*, sold millions of copies, stayed on the pop album chart for sixty-six weeks, peaking at number two, cemented Brown's popularity among blacks, opened a door to white fans, and to this day, many music critics consider *Live at the Apollo* the greatest live album ever made. In 2004, *Live at the Apollo* was one of fifty recordings that year added to the National Recording Registry by the Library of Congress, and *Rolling Stone* magazine ranks the live concert number twenty-five on its list of the 500 Greatest Albums of All Time.

James Brown was born in a one-room shack outside of Barnwell, South Carolina, on May 3, 1933. The cabin was surrounded by pine woods, and two aunts, Estelle and Minnie, were present to help with his birth. At first, his aunts believed he was stillborn: the newborn child was not breathing. When all hope seemed to be lost, Minnie breathed into the infant and the baby Brown let out a scream, announcing his birth to the world. His name went through several changes, from Joe Brown to James Joe Junior Brown, before his parents settled on James Joe Brown, Jr.

James's father's last name was Gardner, but he had adopted the last name of the woman who had raised him, Mattie Brown. After his son's birth, Joe Brown walked nine miles to Barnwell to record his son's name. Brown's mother, Susie Behlings, had been raised in Bamberg, South Carolina. As a young girl, it was Susie's responsibility to clean house, and Susie's mother and sisters often picked on her. When Joe Brown expressed a romantic interest in Susie, her sister Eva objected: no one knew anything about him. Because Eva disapproved, Joe Brown designed a plan to secretly take Susie away and marry her. When the day came, Susie dressed as though she was planning to clean house, but when Brown drove by her home in a Model A Ford, she climbed in the car and left with him. The two married and moved to Barnwell, where their son James Brown was born.

While the law in South Carolina would label the newborn James Brown as black, his rich ethnic heritage drew from multiple races. His grandfather on his father's side had been a Cherokee, and there was Asian and American Indian heritage on his mother's side of the family. "Because of all these different bloodlines," Brown later recalled, "I feel a connection to everybody, not to any special race, but to the human race."

James's father worked harvesting turpentine from the local pine forest and selling it in barrels. He told his son that the pine was his favorite tree: it was always green, no matter what the season. It was a hard living, however, and the Browns were poor.

A turpentine worker in a grove in Georgia in 1941

When James Brown was four, his parents separated, and one of his first memories was of his mother leaving. He remembered his mother and father discussing who would care for him, and recalled not understanding what was happening. Finally, his mother left Brown in the care of his father. He would not see his mother for twenty years. "More than anything else in life," Brown wrote years later, "I would like to have been raised by both parents."

As a young boy, James and his father lived in a series of shacks around Barnwell and Elko in South Carolina. These shacks were small buildings with no running water, no indoor bathrooms, and no electricity. For heat, they burned wood in a stove. The Browns daily diet was always the same, consisting of little more than beans, fatback, syrup, and salad made of the rough greens, called polk salad, which they found growing around their home. This basic diet, along with a lack of available dental care, caused the young James to lose all of his teeth to pyorrhea at an early age.

His father worked a variety of jobs, frequently leaving James at home alone. While he occasionally played with other children, he more often played alone outside. James crawled under the house, dug holes in the ground, and played with what local people called doodle bugs. In later years, he wrote an instrumental called "Doodle Bug." Despite the loneliness of these years, James learned to rely on himself. "No matter what came my way after that—prison, personal problems, government harassment—I had the ability to fall back on myself." James also never forgot what it was like to be poor.

Around this time, James's father gave him a ten-cent

Children sitting on the steps of a ramshackle house in Georgia

harmonica, his first musical instrument. James sang and learned to play songs like "Oh, Susanna" and "John Henry" on his harmonica. He also learned songs by listening to his father sing the blues, though he disliked the blues because the music was downhearted. Even as a young boy, James loved music. Music had the power to make people feel good, no matter what one's circumstances; music had the power to lift people up, even when they had little else in life.

Eventually, Joe Brown left his son in the care of Minnie Walker, James Brown's great aunt. In 1938, James and Walker moved to Augusta, Georgia, a city well-known for vice during the 1930s. Many of the illegal activities had been rooted in the national prohibition of alcohol sales. While the ban on alcohol sales had been lifted nationally, a number of localities in Georgia continued to prohibit alcohol sales. Despite these bans, individual proprietors still sold illegal alcohol, and often, other criminal activities from gambling to prostitution followed.

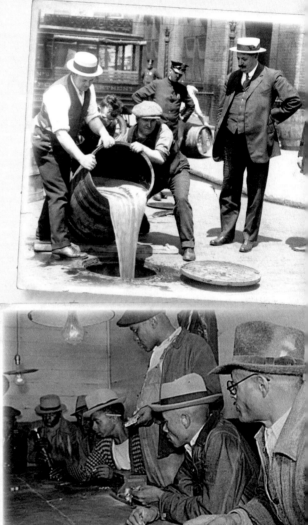

Top photo: Agents pour liquor into a sewer, circa 1921. *Bottom:* Men gambling with their cotton money in a juke joint in 1939.

James and Minnie moved into a primarily black Augusta neighborhood known as the Terry that was also the home of a number of American Chinese and Muslims. "On the other side of the street were all these pretty houses where the White people lived," Brown later wrote. "On our side it was strictly Shantyville." This was James's reality as he grew up. The house they moved into on 944 Twiggs Street belonged to another aunt, Handsome Washington, simply known as Honey. It was a two-story house with as many as fifteen boarders, many of them former farm hands who were out of work. Honey offered these men a place to stay and also bought food and other necessities for poor families in the neighborhood.

Honey supported these men and families by selling gin and operating a house of prostitution. While all of these activities were illegal, Honey paid the local police department to look the other way. Still, the police occasionally harassed Washington, arresting her for short periods of time. Despite the illegal activities, James believed that his aunt—like other poor people in Augusta—was simply doing what was necessary to survive. "Some people call it crime," Brown wrote, "I call it survival."

In Augusta, James was known as Little Junior, the first of many nicknames he would acquire during his lifetime. As a young boy, he helped hide the gin bottles—sold for twenty-five cents a half-pint—beneath the floorboards of his aunt's house, and he gathered loose coal with Honey's grandson, Big Junior, along the railroad tracks to help heat his home. As a boy, James scavenged Augusta for food to make ends meet, even digging through the garbage behind grocery stores to find swollen cans of food. It was a difficult life, and James was continually whipped by one visitor to his aunt's house, named Jack Scott. Still, life with his aunt was home, and even if they were poor, he ate regular meals.

During World War II, Augusta was the home of many soldiers stationed at Camp Gordon. The soldiers brought a great deal of money to Augusta, and James found ways to make loose

change from
them. James ran
errands for the
soldiers, going
for sandwiches
and soda pop.
He also waited
for the moving
convoys on the
Third Level
Canal Bridge
near his home,
where he would
dance for the
soldiers. As
he danced,
the soldiers threw nickels and

New recruits learn to drill in this 1943 photo.

dimes that he and Big Junior took home to Honey. "I started
dancing for nickels and dimes in a real low-life poverty-ridden
environment," Brown later recalled. James also stood outside his
home and worked to bring men who were passing by into the
house for the girls who were prostitutes. Eventually, however, the
presence of the soldiers led local law enforcement to close down
Honey Washington's illegal business.

Ever since he had received his first musical instrument, a
ten-cent harmonica, James had expressed an interest in music.
He learned how to play piano and guitar from local musicians,
including bluesman Tampa Red. James also learned the songs
of the day from the Hit Parade books including Frank Sinatra's
"Saturday Night Is the Loneliest Night of the Week" and Count
Basie's "One O'Clock Jump." When it came to music, James
seemed to have a natural ability.

Once, James's father had brought a pump organ to Aunt
Honey's house, and since it was broken, he used a cheese crate

to prop it up. That evening, when returning home from his job at Eubanks Furniture Store, he saw a crowd gathered in front of Honey's house: men and women from the neighborhood had huddled on the front porch. At first he worried that something was wrong, but after moving through the crowd, he discovered that James was sitting at the organ playing "Coon Shine Baby."

James also learned about music at church. Despite living in a house that supported prostitution and illegal gin, James and his family were devout church attendees. James sang "Old Blind Barnabas" and other gospel songs with Big Junior and a friend named Cornelius, attempting to copy the popular gospel groups like the Golden Gate Quartet. Music in the church was sometimes backed by tambourines and organ, and the congregation clapped hands as they sang along. James even agreed to sweep out the church so that he could play the piano, though not to play gospel songs. As he learned new styles like boogie-woogie piano, he had to make sure that no one overheard him practicing on the church piano: secular music was strictly forbidden.

Although he loved music, as a boy James was more interested in becoming a preacher than a musician. Church, like music, offered comfort and relief from the difficult life that James and many other poor blacks experienced in the South during the 1940s. He watched

The Golden Gate Quartet in 1948

Sweet Daddy Grace is seated in the front. As a boy Brown spent time in lots of different churches. He later drew inspiration from those services, which included lots of handclapping, foot stomping, and fiery preachers who were not afraid to scream, yell, and drop to their knees. "I watched the preachers real close," he later wrote. "Then I'd go home and imitate them."

the minister's every move, and he practiced preaching at home, realizing he had a spiritual gift to reach people. One flamboyant preacher in particular, Bishop C. E. "Sweet Daddy" Grace, captivated young James Brown. Founder of the United Church of Christ for All People, Daddy Grace had arrived in Augusta in 1927. The colorful, prosperity preacher, known for his wavy long hair, long fingernails, and magenta robes over tailored cutback suits, soon built up a large following, attracted in no small part by Grace's powerful brass "shout band." Grace's shout band employed the saxophone, trumpet, and trombone, backed up with piano, drums, tambourine, and scrubbing board. Grace introduced the brass and reed instruments into the church service based on Psalm 150, where David declared "Everything that hath breath [should] praise the Lord. Praise Him with the sound of the trumpet." Looking back later, James Brown realized how his early church experience influenced his approach to music. "I learned rhythm from the band in the House of Prayer." He also later wrote, "I'm sure a lot of my stage show came out of the church."

Louis Armstrong

James also listened and absorbed all the music around him—on the radio, on 78 rpm records, at the movies, and at the local Lenox Theatre. He heard the sounds of jazz, from trumpeter Louis Armstrong to pianist Count Basie, and there was the rhythm and blues of saxophonist Louis Jordan. He first saw Jordan and His Tympany Five in a movie short and was immediately impressed: Jordan created a larger-than-life performance style. Many African American performers were well known and respected, and more than that, many were popular among black and white listeners. Inspired by the music, James entered a talent contest at the Lenox Theatre, singing for the first time in public. The eleven-year-old sang "So Long" loud and clear, winning first prize.

James, however, had more pressing concerns than a possible career in music or the church. After Honey Washington's illegal business was shut down, he moved with his Aunt Minnie to a small place near the University Hospital. Occasionally he saw his father, and when Joe Brown joined the United States Navy, the family received a regular check of $37.50 each month. While this money made life much easier for James, he continued to work odd jobs to make extra money. One of those jobs included shining shoes. At first he freelanced, which meant he shined shoes without a license. He prided himself on his showmanship, developing routines with the shoeshine rag and brushes. While he could make as much as twenty dollars on a Sunday morning shining shoes, operating independently meant running whenever the police showed up. Finally, he joined the Shoeshine King on Broad Street, an establishment that kept seventy cents of every dollar James made.

One aspect that made life in Georgia difficult was segregation. Segregation was a well-established way of life in the American South many years before James was born. Blacks frequently lived in the poorer sections of a town and were treated as second-class citizens. James remembered an early lesson in race relations by watching how his father interacted with local whites. While his father had a temper and sometimes used derogatory terms to describe whites, he always showed respect toward whites when he was in their presence. To young James, his father's behavior seemed insincere: he could not respect anyone who allowed themselves to be bullied by other people—whatever the racial background.

James disliked the fact that a white man could call a black man by his first name, but a black man would always have to call a white man by his last name preceded by mister. Starting at a young age, James believed that respect was an important virtue.

A 1943 "Colored Waiting Room" sign at a bus station in Rome, Georgia

In the 1930s and 1940s, much of America remained
heavily segregated. In many American towns and cities,
this meant that blacks and whites lived in separate
neighborhoods. In the American South, however,
segregation ran much deeper. In the South, blacks were
frequently denied basic rights, including the right to vote.
Blacks were not allowed to eat at the same restaurants
as whites, and they were not allowed to ride in the same
railroad cars. With public facilities, blacks and whites
had separate drinking fountains, restrooms, libraries, and
schools. Many laws that separated blacks and whites,
known as Jim Crow laws, had been established after the
Civil War.

Part of what made segregation so difficult was that
"separate but equal" was rarely equal. Black schools, for
instance, were frequently makeshift buildings, and
public funding for black schools was often much less
than funding for white schools. The black experience
was further impacted by the Great Depression of the
1930s. During these years, as many as one-third of all
Americans were unemployed at one time and, generally,
these unemployment numbers were higher in the black
community. Even after the Depression during the 1940s,
many black people remained under economic hardship.

Segregation and poverty also created a racial divide.
Augusta, like many Southern towns, had a local chapter
of the Ku Klux Klan, an organization that persecuted
blacks. The Klan held parades that marched through
the Terry that James and other blacks attended: he
never thought very much about why these parades were
being held or what they represented. Attending was just
something everyone did. As with Klan rallies in Augusta,
the racial divide defined many aspects of life in the South.
Traveling minstrel shows featured comics and musicians

A Klan gathering

who darkened their faces with burnt cork, performing in blackface. Even black performers sometimes spread burnt cork on their faces to give the impression of darker skin. During World War II, this racial divide was even evident in the treatment of white German prisoners of war (POWs). The federal government housed German POWs at the Augusta Arsenal, and even while they were in prison, they received better treatment than the local black population. Eventually the prisoners were allowed to work

Boys and girls singing at a segregated
Georgia school in 1941

on local farms, receiving eighty cents per day: this was more than James's father could earn on most days, and more than many black farmhands could earn.

After Joe Brown's Navy check stopped coming, James's day-to-day life grew more difficult. In school, he had been sent home for having insufficient clothes. "I was nine years old before I had my first store-bought underwear," Brown recalled, "my clothes having been made out of sacks and things like that." In the seventh grade, James dropped out of school. He began stealing hubcaps and other items to buy the things he needed, and he started to hang out with a gang. Despite his behavior, he nonetheless had a code: he never stole from African Americans, and he never allowed his cousin, Big Junior, to become involved. He frequently gave clothing and other items he stole to other people who had too little. One time, he stole a number of baseball gloves and distributed them to local kids. Eventually, however, James was caught.

One night James went out with several friends, stealing clothes from parked cars on Broad Street in Augusta. Later that evening, two of his friends got caught, but James got away. The next day the police were looking for "James Brown," and when they tried to pick him up at the shoeshine stand, James ran from the police and eventually got away. They chased him a second time, and once again, he outmaneuvered the police. The third time, however, James ran into a dead end alley and soon found himself surrounded by squad cars. He was taken to the police station, fingerprinted, and put in jail: James was charged with four counts of breaking into the automobiles.

Even though James understood that he had broken the law, he realized that he—as a poor African American—would receive a harsher sentence than a white person from the middle class. He also realized that when blacks were not given an education, many would end up exactly where he ended up. "If you don't allow a man to get an education, don't put him in jail for being dumb. That's what they did in Augusta—they sent me to prison for being dumb." On June 13, 1949, Judge Grover C. Anderson handed down James's sentence for the four charges against him: he was sentenced to eight to sixteen years in jail. At the age of sixteen, James was on his way to the Georgia Juvenile Training Institute in Rome.

Cars parked along Broad Street in Augusta, Georgia, in 1936

Brown in 1955

Chapter Two

PLEASE, PLEASE, PLEASE

On June 14, 1952, after three years and one day in prison, nineteen-year-old James Brown was released early for good behavior. As part of his early release, however, he would remain on probation for several years. Prison in Rome and later Toccoa, Georgia, had been difficult, but James had filled his time, working in the laundry room during the week, and playing baseball and singing gospel with other inmates during his spare time. Under the terms of his probation, he would have to maintain a job and have a stable place to live to keep from returning to prison. He found a job washing cars and cleaning up at Lawson Motors, an Oldsmobile dealership in Toccoa.

In prison, James had received a new nickname, Music Box, and he had also met a local musician, Bobby Byrd. When James first arrived in Toccoa, Byrd's family provided him with a temporary place to stay. "When Bobby went and got James out of prison when he was a boy," singer Vicki Anderson who later worked with both Byrd and Brown said, "[and] when he brought him to live in his home as his brother, that was something you can't buy." Byrd was also a member of a vocal group that began as gospel singers but soon branched out to the rhythm and blues style that was becoming popular in the late 1940s and early 1950s. As the Gospel Starlighters, Byrd's group sang gospel; as the Avons, Byrd's group imitated the popular groups of the day, including the Dells and the Moonglows. James, meanwhile, had joined the Community Choir at Trinity Church in Toccoa, and he had also formed a quartet from the church, the Ever Ready Gospel Singers. When Byrd asked James to join his gospel/rhythm and blues group, he hesitated. He was happy singing gospel, and since he also played baseball locally, he had little extra time. The Starlighters and Avons would have to wait until another time.

Even as a gospel singer, however, James was determined to become better known. He obtained permission from a local radio station to use WLET's studio, allowing the Ever Ready Gospel Singers to record "His Eye Is on the Sparrow" on tape. The gospel hymn dated back to 1905 and had been made famous by singer Ethel Waters. It served as a favorite in many black churches. The

Ever Ready Gospel Singers then converted the tape recording into an acetate, a non-label recording. It was the first time James had recorded a song. Traveling to Nashville, the singers asked a disc jockey on radio station WLAC to play the record, and while the disc jockey admitted that he liked the recording, he refused to play it.

Ethel Waters

James decided to join Byrd's group in late 1952 or early 1953. The other members included Bobby Byrd, Sylvester Keels, Doyle Oglesby, Fred Pulliam, Nash Knox, and Baby Roy Scott. The band rehearsed each Sunday in the living room of Byrd's house. At first, Brown's addition was awkward: his vocal style was rough, while the group sang smooth harmony. Over time, however, all of the voices began to work better together. They practiced popular songs of the day by the Dominoes, Orioles, and Clovers. At first, the band focused on vocal arrangements, performing without instruments. "When we saw all the girls screaming for groups like Hank Ballard & The Midnighters," Byrd later recalled, "we thought, 'Oh, so this is what we want to do!'"

While many local friends and family members enjoyed the Avons's style, local churches disliked the new music. Byrd's grandmother, who owned the house the group practiced in, considered rhythm and blues sinful. If gospel music was God's music, then rhythm and blues, a music that incited kids to dance, was from the devil. Earlier, many blacks had rejected the blues for the same reason. Instead of focusing on religious themes, the blues and R&B often focused on relationships. Among young listeners, however, rhythm and blues found a receptive audience.

The music that Brown and his friends performed developed against a backdrop of gospel, doo-wop, and rhythm and blues in the 1940s and early 1950s. The term rhythm and blues, often shortened to R&B, was first used by Jerry Wexler in *Billboard Magazine* in 1948; the following year, *Billboard* replaced its Harlem Hit Parade chart with an R&B chart. Previously, most black music had been referred to as race records. R&B combined blues and jazz, two musical styles that had originated and been developed by black musicians. R&B spread quickly in urban centers and represented the black experience in post–World War II America. R&B would also serve as a foundation for the development of both rock & roll in the mid-1950s and soul music in the late 1950s and early 1960s.

R&B focused on songs more than musical improvising, and the songs were grounded in a steady backbeat. In 4/4 time, amounting to four beats to a measure, R&B placed an emphasis on the second and fourth beats. This would also be true of rock & roll. A basic R&B band included a bassist, drummer, saxophonist, and pianist. Frequently, R&B bands recorded for small labels like Chess, King, and Imperial. Early influential R&B performers included Louis Jordan, Charles Brown, Roy Milton, and Ruth Brown. Whether in live performance or on records, the R&B beat created movement that propelled teenagers to get up and dance.

Bandleader Louis Jordan in 1954

James attended a number of R&B shows in Greenville, South Carolina, including performances by Bill Doggett, the Clovers, and Hank Ballard and the Midnighters. "The Midnighters were the first professionals we'd ever seen. We traveled sixty miles to the Greenville Textile Hall and stood down front for their show." Louis Jordan, the most popular R&B performer of the 1940s, would also exert a great deal of influence over James. Jordan sang and played saxophone, and James admired his energy and sense of style. Jordan's signature song, "Caledonia," became one of the biggest R&B hits, reaching number one on the Harlem Hit Parade in the 1940s.

Despite the disapproval of Byrd's grandmother, the Avons persevered and soon played their first live show in Toccoa at Bill's Rendezvous Club. Around this time, the band experienced a minor crisis, finding themselves temporarily without a name: another local band was also called the Avons. Name or no name, Byrd and James's band began playing at local clubs, often referred to as juke joints because of the jukeboxes that supplied music to customers when a band was not present. At this point, James, Byrd, and the other band members were primarily a vocal group, relying on no more than a piano for background accompaniment. The band traveled from town to town making a name for itself, cramming the members and musical equipment into a 1941 Ford station wagon that they rented from Guy Wilson who attended the same church.

While James loved performing, he nonetheless felt conflicted about his future. He also loved sports and was a pitcher on the Toccoa baseball team. He dreamed of becoming a professional baseball player, but after injuring his back and knee, he knew he had less of a chance. Instead of feeling frustrated, however, the injuries clarified his ambition: "After that, I threw all my energies into making it as a singer, and pushed the band and Mr. Byrd harder than I ever had before."

Even early on, the band experienced personality conflicts, and these conflicts seemed to follow James to every band he would ever join or form. A number of members worried that James and Byrd, the two lead singers, garnered more attention than everyone else; a number of members wanted to break up the band. This had been the same issue that had broken up the Ever Ready Gospel Singers. Brown convinced the band that they—as musicians and performers—were just getting started. Now was the time to work harder, not break up. During the discussion, the band also decided that a new name was needed, something that captured the excitement of the group's live performances. Drawing inspiration from another local band called the Torches, they decided to call themselves the Flames. Later, they became the Famous Flames.

James and the Famous Flames worked hard, playing a string of one-nighters. Despite a positive reception, the band still lacked something extra to separate it from other bands, something that gave the Flames a personal trademark. One way to do this was to write original material. At the time, however, the Famous Flames—like many other bands of the era—focused on learning the latest radio hits. A friend simply known as Williams suggested that when audiences attended a Famous Flames show and applauded, they were applauding the song, not the band. Unless the Flames had its own songs, the group would never reach a larger audience.

James had written songs before, but he had never considered original material important. Now, he turned his attention to writing something unique, a showcase for his vocal style, and a song that audiences would associate with the Famous Flames. Thinking of the repeated phrase of "please" in the Orioles's "Baby, Please Don't Go," James formed the words to a new song and etched out the melody on the piano. The following day he taught it to the Famous Flames, and soon, the new song became a showstopper: audiences loved it. While the lyric of the song was simple, and the word please was repeated many times, a performance of "Please, Please, Please" could last up to forty minutes, with James pleading with a make-believe woman to let him come back home.

It was during the performance of "Please, Please, Please" that James developed a dramatic routine that became more elaborate over time, and eventually became the centerpiece of his live shows for the rest of his performing life. After pleading for redemption, he would fall to his knees and then, getting up, turn his back on the audience and walk into the shadows. At this moment, a band member would hang a cape on James's shoulders, serving as a comforter to his dejected friend. As though recovering from his dejection, James would throw the cape off and continue to plead with his love to allow his return. Even within one performance of "Please, Please, Please," the cape routine could be repeated many times. The display of emotion was worthy of many of the scenes James had grown up with in Georgia churches.

While the song was still two years away from being recorded, "Please, Please, Please" gave the Famous Flames exactly what they needed at the time: a little something extra to separate themselves from other groups. The song, over time, would also draw the attention of the recording industry.

On June 19, 1953, a little more than a year after his release from prison, James married Velma Warren at Trinity Church in Toccoa. They had met when he performed with the Ever Ready Gospel Singers: the group frequently sang at her church, Mount Zion Baptist Church. The idea of home and marriage appealed to James, partly because he had never had a steady home or family. By starting a family of his own, James could be the kind of father that he never had growing up. "I didn't just want to be a daddy—I wanted to be a strong one, to be there for my kids, no matter what the personal sacrifice might be." Unfortunately, it was difficult for James to be the ideal husband and father, because he spent so much time away from home performing music. He would realize over time that as important as family was, becoming successful would require sacrifices including very little home life.

In January 1956, Brown and the Famous Flames were approached by Ralph Bass of King Records. The group was performing at a place called Sawyers Lake, outside of Milledgeville, Georgia. Bass sat in the corner, a lone white face in a black crowd, and during an intermission, he introduced himself to the band. He asked whether the band had original material, and then told the band that he wanted them to record for King Records. King, a small regional label based in Cincinnati, had been founded by Syd Nathan in 1943. While King specialized in country music, the label also issued R&B records on its Queen and Federal imprints. Unlike many record labels of the era, King controlled all aspects of a recording, from mastering to manufacturing and distributing new singles and albums. Bass was offering the Famous Flames a chance to reach a larger audience by making a record, and they jumped at the chance. "From then on," Brown recalled, "everything happened very quickly."

After the initial meeting with Bass, however, the Famous Flames heard nothing from the record label. Early in 1956, they were performing at clubs in Florida, barely making ends meet, when they received a call from the record label: King wanted the group in Cincinnati right away to record a single. James and the Famous Flames left Florida, driving an old station wagon from Tampa to Macon, Georgia, where they stopped to get more money. From Macon, the band began the second, six-hundred-mile leg of the trip, driving all night to Cincinnati: it would be the first time anyone in the Famous Flames had traveled outside of the South. When they arrived, a representative from King took the band to a hotel called the Manse. Instead of sleeping, however, James and the band toured the King facilities, and a recording session was scheduled for the following day.

Nothing, however, went as planned. When Brown and the band arrived at the studio the next day, they learned that the recording had been postponed. Singer Hank Ballard had arrived unexpectedly, and all personnel at King were occupied

Hank Ballard and the Midnighters

with a meeting. The following day, the recording was postponed once again when singer Little Willie John arrived at the studio for a recording session. Even though the Famous Flames had signed a recording contract with King, other groups that had been on the label longer still had priority over resources.

Finally, on February 4, 1956, Brown and the Famous Flames occupied the studio for their first recording session with the label. Several people were in the control booth including the president Syd Nathan, the musical director Gene Redd, and the engineer who had signed the band, Ralph Bass. James disliked the idea of a musical director: he knew the Famous Flames's music better than anyone else from performing it on the road, and he did not want anyone else dictating vocals or instrumental arrangements. When the recording tape started rolling, Brown and the band performed "Please, Please, Please" in the same style they used on stage.

When the Flames were only halfway through the recording, however, Nathan stopped the recording. He objected to everything about the song: the words, the style of the Famous Flames, and Brown's sung repetitions. He could not understand the rawness of the music, and he could not understand why anyone would repeat the same phrase—please—over and over. After complaining that he hated the song and after asking James to change the lyrics, Nathan walked out, leaving James and the Famous Flames wondering what would happen next. Here the band was, recording in a professional studio for the first time, and their very first session seemed to have come to an end after only half a song. They waited anxiously while Redd left the studio to talk to Nathan. When he returned, he gave the green light to continue recording. That day, James and the

Syd Nathan

Flames recorded "Please, Please, Please," "Why Do You Love Me Like You Do," "I Feel That Old Feeling Coming On," and "I Don't Know."

Still, no one was sure what would happen next with these recordings. The biggest concern was that Nathan would simply refuse to release "Please, Please, Please." Brown's manager, Clint Brantley, phoned Nathan every day until he finally said that he would release the single, even though he believed that it would not sell. On March 3, 1956, King issued "Please, Please, Please," and the song did exactly what Nathan said it would not do: it began to sell rapidly. "I was working ten hours a day for less than 100 dollars a month," Brown later recalled. "I love that song ('Please, Please, Please') like I love one of my relatives. You know, if it wasn't for that song, I'd still be a janitor."

Nathan changed the name of the band twice as he pressed more records, first to James Brown with the Famous Flames and finally to James Brown and the Famous Flames. Eventually, the name of the group was changed to James Brown and His Famous Flames, reigniting jealousy within the group.

While the other band members complained, James believed that the name change was justified. He wrote "Please, Please, Please," designed the stage show, sang lead vocals, and oversaw most aspects of the group's career. If audiences were primarily coming to see the person who wrote and sang "Please, Please, Please," then the name James Brown and His Famous Flames was justified.

The King Record Label

He did worry about hurting Bobby Byrd's feelings—Byrd had supported him right after James's release from prison—but he believed that even Byrd understood that the change was deserved.

The change, however, was about more than a hit song called "Please, Please, Please," and about more than James wanting to see his name on a big city marquee. James simply had more talent and ambition than the other Famous Flames, and he knew that the group's lack of drive and creativity would hold him back. Quickly, "Please, Please, Please" climbed the R&B chart, reaching number five: it also became James's first million seller. The Famous Flames had played small clubs all over the South, and while they were surviving on the road, they were hardly prosperous. From James's point of view, he and the band were at a crossroads. They could continue to play small venues throughout the South, building a regional reputation, or they could take advantage of a hit single and try to reach a national audience. At twenty-three years old, James Brown was ready to introduce himself to the world.

Brown back-stage at the Apollo, 1964

Chapter Three

LIVE AT THE APOLLO

By the early 1960s, Brown had achieved moderate success as an R&B singer. Starting in 1959, he had placed a string of singles on the R&B charts, and songs like "Try Me" (1959) had also reached the *Billboard* Hot 100. As a live performer, he maintained a busy schedule on the East Coast, including his first performance at the prestigious Apollo Theater in Harlem, New York. Despite this success, Brown wanted more. He wanted to push his music in new directions, but he believed that his record label and the musicians around him were holding him back. He also wanted to reach a broader audience, one that went beyond his loyal base of black supporters.

Brown's problems with his career dated back to his success with "Please, Please, Please" in 1956. While "Please, Please, Please" seemed like the beginning of a new phase for Brown and the Famous Flames, several problems plagued the group. Wanting to capitalize on "Please, Please, Please," King Records haphazardly

released a series of singles starting with
"I Don't Know" and "I Feel That Old
Feeling Coming On." A month later,
King issued "No, No, No" and "Hold
My Baby's Hand." Even as "Please, Please,
Please" was still climbing the charts, the
release of so many other singles during a
short span of time seemed to confuse the
listening public. Despite Brown's respect
for King's president, he worried that
Nathan's marketing of the group's singles
was chaotic.

Brown was also less than happy about
the material he was recording. The
record company wanted another "Please,
Please, Please," and King pushed the
Famous Flames toward familiar R&B
material. At the beginning of 1957, King
issued "Chonnie-on-Chon," a song that
sounded very similar to the singles being
released at the time by rock singer Little
Richard. James tried to offer original
interpretations of the songs he was asked
to sing, but he wanted to develop new
musical territory. On top of resistance
from Nathan and King, even the
Famous Flames seemed reluctant to try
anything new. The group remained more
comfortable with the kind of songs they
had been performing live. James, tasting
his first real success with "Please, Please,
Please," wanted to work harder than ever
and take chances: everyone around him,
he believed, was holding him back.

The Famous Flames in 1956

These tensions were further aggravated by the jealousy that continued to undermine the Famous Flames. As before, many members within the group believed that Brown received too much attention. When the name of the group was changed to James Brown and His Famous Flames, jealousy bubbled over. Even though the band was now playing better jobs and beginning to gain momentum in the Northeast, most of the group's members were unhappy. Early in 1957, the band's booking company, Universal, called everyone into the office to discuss the future of the group. Everyone, except for James, quit the group and returned to Toccoa, Georgia.

For many performers, this might have been a career-ending setback. Brown was disappointed, but he had no intention of going back home: this was his life. He knew that he could find a new band, but he had other concerns that went deeper. He seemed to work harder than ever, performing as many as 350 engagements a year, but he was still struggling for recognition. As dynamic as Brown was as a performer, his success, so far, had been inconsistent. While he was a leading voice in the transition from R&B to soul music, he still needed an artistic and popular triumph that would place him at the top of the entertainment ladder.

One thing that had always displeased Brown about the recording process was that no matter how well he sang, his vocals lacked the excitement of a live performance. "People who couldn't get to one of my shows," Brown said, "especially an Apollo show, missed that special thing that always happened live." To Brown, the solution to capturing that energy was the same as the solution to creating an artistic and popular triumph: record a live performance of a James Brown show at the Apollo Theater.

Brown had attended his first show at the Apollo on his first trip to New York City in 1956 or 1957. The price of admission was for the entire day, and Brown and the Flames had seen the Dells and the Cadillacs that day. For black entertainers in the 1950s,

Brown understood that the Apollo was the place that separated the merely good from the great. The audience that filled the auditorium was known as "the toughest audience in the world." Later, some people also recalled Brown performing at the Apollo on Amateur Night during the 1950s, though he always denied the story.

Located at 253 West 125th Street in Harlem, the Apollo Hall had been established as a dance hall by General Edward Ferrero in 1872. The architect George Keister designed a new building on the same sight in 1913-14, and the building was renamed the Hartig and Seaman's New (Burlesque) Theater. Following the Harlem Renaissance, a black movement in the arts during the 1920s and 1930s, the rechristened Apollo Theater began to focus on African American performers. Jazz singer Ella Fitzgerald

The Apollo Theater between 1946 and 1948

Sarah Vaughan in 1946

appeared in 1934, and by the 1950s—when James Brown
first visited the theater—the theater hosted a long list of black
performers including Johnny Otis, the Dixie Hummingbirds,
and Sarah Vaughan. For a black performer, the Apollo was a
proving ground.

In 1959 Brown made his first appearance as a professional
entertainer at the Apollo. The show included Hank Ballard and
the Midnighters, the Upsetters, and the headliner, Little Willie
John. Preparing for the show was trying for Brown—he had fired
a second version of the Famous Flames for a variety of infractions.
He quickly put together a third version of the band that included
one of the original Famous Flames, Bobby Byrd. A reviewer of
the show noted in *Variety*, that the, "group, led by James Brown,
almost blows out the walls to the obvious delight of the audience."
Even after putting together a topnotch band, the schedule at the
Apollo was tough. The booking lasted for a week, while the daily
schedule—starting at 11:00 a.m.—included six and seven shows.
Brown recalled, "you ate there, slept there, and kept rehearsing
there when you were not on stage."

Brown also met a long lost acquaintance following the last
of these shows. He had a room at the Theresa and was getting
ready to move on to Washington, DC, for shows at the Howard.
A knock came at the door, and he told the person to come in. He
imagined it was his manager, or maybe someone sending flowers.
Someone came in, stood behind him, and remained silent. Brown
waited for the person to speak, and after several moments of
silence, he turned around: soon he realized that it was his mother
who he had not seen in twenty years. When she smiled, he saw
that she had lost all of her teeth: he was unable to think of any
reply except to offer to have her teeth fixed. Without speaking
she hugged him, and he kissed her. From then on, Brown would
occasionally visit her when he was in New York City. He would
make four other appearances at the Apollo, finally appearing as a
headliner, before deciding to record a live show at the theater in
the fall of 1962.

Brown decided to ask for the opinion of those around him about recording a live show. Everyone, except for Bobby Byrd, believed it was a bad idea. There were many reasons not to record a live show. Live recordings had to deal with audience noise, and the overall sound quality was often inferior to a studio recording. There were many other unpredictable factors including mistakes made by musicians, audience noise, and technical mishaps. The more resistance Brown met with, however, the more determined he was to follow through.

Nathan at King Records also objected. A live recording would only include songs that had already been available as singles, and he was sure that no one would buy an album full of old songs. Likewise, radio stations would refuse to play old songs, hurting the promotion of a new album. Nathan also worried that someone in the audience might say something inappropriate. Finally, the King president delivered his verdict: his record label would not pay for a live recording.

Brown continued to hold on to the idea of a live recording nonetheless. Perhaps, he thought, if he continued to do well as a performer, he would gain the kind of clout that would prompt his label to pay for a live recording. On October 19, 1961, he had appeared on Dick Clark's *American Bandstand*, and now he was scheduled to appear on the influential show a second time. Brown also toured through Ohio with a number of performers from Motown Records, an up-and-coming record label that produced popular groups like the Supremes. Both the invitation to perform on Clark's program and the Motown tour signaled that Brown's appeal had the potential to reach a broader audience, including white teenagers.

An original ticket from 1962

Teens dancing on Dick Clark's *American Bandstand* in 1961

Nathan, however, remained unconvinced, and Brown proceeded without his label's approval. He talked to his full-time manager, Jack "Pops" Bart, about recording at the Apollo. He wanted to record the album during upcoming shows at the Apollo during the week of October 19. He also instructed Bart to change his contract arrangement with the Apollo.

Originally, the Apollo had paid Brown a percentage of the profit from the shows. As Brown became more popular at the theater, he believed he had the chance to make more and more money there. Instead, one of the owners of the Apollo, Frank Schiffman, changed the arrangement without consulting Brown: now he would only receive a flat fee. Angry, Brown came up with a new plan: he would rent the Apollo, allowing him to oversee all aspects of the performance as well as make a better profit. Bart worried that the Apollo would not accept this deal, but Brown refused to return to the theater unless Schiffman accepted the new arrangement. Although Schiffman resisted the change, he finally agreed.

Bart also pursued the necessary arrangements for a live recording, though Nathan remained set against it: Brown could record a live album if he wanted, but King would not pay for it. Finally, Brown told Nathan that he would pay for the recording himself. At the time, Brown later recalled, $5,700 was a lot of money to him, "which was every bit of coin I could lay my hands on at the time." Eventually, Nathan agreed that a live recording would be a good idea, and even began making suggestions for the recording. Brown, however, was determined to record the show his way: Nathan, after all, still refused to support the project with money.

Besides Brown's struggle with the record label, the recording at the Apollo took place against a dramatic backdrop of world politics that added extra tension to the concert: during the month of October in 1962, many worried that the United States was on the brink of war with the Soviet Union.

Ever since the end of World War II, the Soviet Union (USSR) and the United States had engaged in a Cold War. Instead of military conflict, the US and USSR stationed troops around the world and stockpiled nuclear weapons, attempting to maintain parity with one another. Often, these maneuvers caused tensions between the countries. On the eve of Brown's recording of his Apollo show, these tensions were at perhaps their highest level since World War II.

In September 1962, the USSR transported nuclear weapons to Cuba, a Russian ally. When the US discovered that the weapons had been transported to Cuba in October, the government believed that they formed an immediate threat: Cuba was only ninety miles away from the Florida coast. President Kennedy demanded that the weapons be removed immediately, and the US military was placed on high alert. Initially, Soviet premier Nikita Khrushchev refused to remove the weapons, stating that the USSR was within its rights. On October 22, two days before the Apollo show, President Kennedy appeared on national television, informing the American public of the crisis. He also announced a naval blockade of Cuba, a strategic move that would prevent more Russian military equipment from arriving in Cuba.

Strikers for peace demonstrate near the United Nations building in New York City.

On the day of October 24, when audiences lined up around the block of the Apollo for Brown's concert, the gathering crowd was well aware of the seriousness of the Cuban Missile Crisis. Many worried that if tensions overflowed, a nuclear war was imminent. These concerns weighed heavy on the minds of many Americans, and heavy on the minds of the New Yorkers who filled the Apollo that day in Harlem.

Preparations for the show, however, continued. Since Brown had rented the Apollo, he was able to include many personal touches at the theater. As with his stage show, he would add a touch of class, dressing the concession workers in uniforms and the ushers in tuxedoes. Everyone had to look his or her best and be on his or her best behavior. "James was very intense because he was booking the Apollo himself," Bobby Byrd later recalled. "He had everyone in tuxedos." From being seated to the live show, Brown focused on the overall quality of the concert experience.

With Brown's money on the line, he knew that everything had to go better than great on October 24th. It had to be perfect. Three of the shows that day would be recorded, which meant that the record producers could use the best sounding song from each show. Even with three shows to choose from, Brown still knew that certain things had to go right—the choice of songs, the audience response, and, perhaps most importantly, the overall energy level. Hal Neely, who worked at King, rented portable sound equipment from A-1 Sound in New York, and together with Chuck Seitz, set up a series of microphones to record the band and the audience response. Everything was ready. After a series of opening acts, announcer Fats Gonder presented his famous introduction of Brown:

So now ladies and gentlemen it is star time, are you ready for star time? Thank you and thank you very kindly. It is indeed a great pleasure to present to you at this particular time, national and international[ly] known as the hardest working man in show business . . .

James Brown performs with The Famous Flames at the Apollo Theater in 1964.

When Brown hit the stage, everything fell into place: the house was full, the mood was right, and the band was cooking. It was going to be a good night.

Even with everything working in Brown's favor, little problems developed along the way. He noticed a number of small things, things that usually would not have mattered. A missed note, an audience member screaming at the wrong moment—all of these things now seemed magnified because the show was being recorded.

One audience member, for instance, was loud and clear on the recorded tape. She was an older woman, positioned below one of the microphones, and quite enthusiastic. While this showed the excitement for the live performance, she continued to shout profanities that could never appear on the final record. Brown guessed the woman must have been seventy-five, and each time she shouted out a new phrase, he worried that another song would be unusable. At another point, she screamed during one of the more serious songs, causing the audience to laugh at an inappropriate time. When Brown and the band listened to the tape after the first show, they laughed—they could hear everything the woman said. Despite the humor, they realized something would have to be done.

Finally, Neely approached the woman in the audience, offering her ten dollars to remain at the next three shows. Brown and Neely wanted the woman's yells and screams on the tape, but they did not want her profanity to be audible. For the next shows, then, they moved the microphone further away from her. "She brought the house down," Byrd recalled, "she was a big part of the album."

Once recorded, even Nathan at King wanted to release the album quickly. Problems ensued, though: Brown also wanted to release it, but he wanted Nathan to pay him back for his $5,700 investment. The four tape reels from the four shows also required work in order to create an album that flowed like a typical James Brown concert. When *Live at the Apollo* was ready in January

1963, Brown, Byrd, and Nathan discussed which songs should be released as singles. Brown suggested selling the album itself and forgetting the singles, while Nathan insisted that all the money he had ever made in the record business was from singles.

Brown solved this dilemma with an innovation that may have been new at the time: no space was put in-between the album cuts. His logic for this unusual approach was simple: if radio stations wanted to play part of the album, the station would have to play at least one half of it. Nathan, on the other hand, still wanted to release singles from the album, but he wanted to wait and see what the radio stations were playing. Brown's strategy, however, worked better than even he imagined. When King called radio stations to find out which cuts were being played from the album, they learned that many stations were playing the entire thirty-minute album. Often, R&B stations played the first half of the album, inserted a commercial, and then played the remainder of the album.

The success of *Live at the Apollo* went beyond the earlier success of singles like "Please, Please, Please" and "Try Me." That the album did well on the R&B chart was no surprise: Brown had released a string of singles since 1959 that had marked out a place on the R&B charts. What no one expected was that *Live at the Apollo* would reach number two on the *Billboard* Top Pop Album chart, and remain there for sixty-six weeks. Since the Top Pop Album chart represented a broad range of markets, the chart position revealed that Brown's music was reaching beyond the black community. With *Live at the Apollo*, he was reaching all Americans.

James Brown sings into a vintage microphone while performing in New York City in 1962

Chapter Four

FROM SOUL TO FUNK

Critics and fans loved *Live at the Apollo*, and Brown was satisfied with his accomplishment: the album pushed Brown's career to a new level. He now reached a broader audience, an audience of white and black listeners, and each new single became a hit. After years of effort, including the sacrifice of family life and the loss of the original Famous Flames, Brown had seemingly reached the success he had always strived towards: at the age of thirty, James Brown, born a poor boy in Depression-era Georgia, was a successful national entertainer.

Brown, however, had no intentions of slowing down. If he was determined to reach the top, he was just as determined to stay there. Looking at his rise to popularity, Brown told a magazine writer during the mid-1960s:

I guess I should get used to it, by now. But while
I'm singing, while I answer to my public, I can't
help but think how the whole thing was difficult
to achieve. Now I am a star . . . yet all this
seems so remote in a sense, like a dream, like an
impossible dream. In the back of my mind, there's
still the fighting, the difficult days I've known
and which I simply can't forget, which I'm not
ready to forget.

He continued to perform more than three hundred concerts
a year and actively promoted his career by visiting radio stations
for interviews with disc jockeys whenever he was in town for a
show. In the mid-1960s, Alan Leeds worked as a disc jockey; later
he worked for James Brown Productions. He remembered Brown
coming by his radio station in 1965 for an interview: "Within
an hour I not only had the interview but a series of personalized
jingles for my radio show." Brown's philosophy was simple: make
the disc jockey your friend because, "'Friends will play your
records forever.'"

Artistically, however, Brown realized that *Live at the Apollo*
was only a stopping point along the way. Even as he performed
old favorites on stage in live settings, he always heard musical
sounds in his head—visions of new ways of playing R&B and
soul music. Brown was always looking toward the next song,
the next riff, and the next big thing. He was always trying to
understand how to find the right arrangement for the right
musicians in the studio, to transfer what was in his head to
a recording.

With the artistic and commercial success of *Live at the Apollo*,
Brown was ready to move forward. Despite his success, though,
a number of complications prevented him from acting on his
new ideas. The biggest complication was his relationship with
his record label King. Nathan, the label's president, had been

ill and unable to focus his full attention on King; furthermore, Brown believed that Nathan's ideas about the music business were behind the times. It was possible that these problems could have been overcome as they had in the past, but Brown also believed that the label was underpaying his recording royalties. With his dissatisfaction growing, Brown left the label for Smash Records in the spring of 1964, a label owned by Mercury.

Leaving King, however, proved more difficult than Brown imagined. While recording new material for Smash, King continued to release a number of backlogged and older recordings by Brown. Before Smash could actively sponsor new recordings, Nathan brought a lawsuit against Brown, claiming he was still under contract with King. Mercury countered with another lawsuit, and the court battle between the two record labels over Brown would drag out for almost a year. Initially, Brown continued to release singles for Mercury, but eventually the court ordered that all vocal releases on Smash stop (instrumental releases could continue). In essence, the court order placed Brown's career in limbo. "Just when I should have been reaping the rewards of ten years of hard work," Brown wrote, "I was stuck." Brown continued to tour and perform, but it would be a year before he could release new material.

Before the court injunction prevented new Brown recordings from Smash, he released one of the biggest hits of his career on the label. "Out of Sight" climbed to number twenty-four on both the *Billboard* R&B and Hot 100 charts, continuing—like *Live at the Apollo*—to show that he was reaching both a white and black audience. "Out of Sight" also signaled the first glimpse of a new artistic direction, building on the musical foundation of soul, but developing a sound unlike anything else on the radio in 1964. "Out of Sight" starts with a bass guitar, providing a short introduction before Brown begins singing. The bass, guitar, and drum arrangement was enriched by a horn section, and together they provided a steady groove that underpinned Brown's vocal.

Whereas a song's melody line had remained important in much of soul music, Brown focused more heavily on rhythm with "Out of Sight." This simplified the overall song structure, allowing his vocals to play against the steady pulse of the bass and drums. The rhythm itself became more complex and layered, a method Brown had often used in concert. His use of polyrhythm was similar to the use of rhythm in traditional African culture, a sound that West African slaves had imported to America in the 1600s and 1700s.

Brown seemed unsure of how to define his new musical direction. "It's a little beyond me right now," he told a radio audience. "I can't really understand it. It's the only thing on the market that sounds like it."

Brown's musical direction was fueled by the addition of several new band members he hired in 1964-65. Nat Jones worked as the band's musical director, while the Parker brothers, Maceo and Melvin, played saxophone and drums respectively. Jimmy Nolan was known as "Chank" because of his rhythm guitar strum, while John "Jabo" Starks also played drums. Even with a large number of players, arrangements by Brown and Jones produced a clean, muscular sound. Perhaps from performing regularly on the road, the players seemed to have a telepathic sense of one another.

For the Parker brothers, playing with Brown was a dream realized. Melvin Parker remembered what it was like to join the band:

> James had wanted me to join the year before, but I was still in school. The next time he came through town I was ready, and I had Maceo with me. I mean our bags were packed. Somehow, I had the nerve to tell James I wouldn't go without Maceo. Maceo played tenor [saxophone], but James needed a baritone—and Maceo carried one of those, too. We were in.

Brown performing onstage at the Santa Monica Civic Auditorium in Santa Monica, California

Brown relied on his band to interpret his new material, to aid him in realizing his vision on the road and in the studio. Often, he sketched directions to his players and musical directors, allowing them to fill in the details. Alfred "Pee Wee" Ellis recalled Brown's musical direction:

> James called me in . . . his dressing room after a gig, said we were going to record soon and for me to have the band ready. He grunted the rhythm, a bass line, to me. I wrote the rhythm down on a piece of paper. There were no notes. I had to translate it. . . . James gave us a lot to go by. You got a musical palette from hearing him, from seeing his body movement and facial expressions, seeing him dance and from being up there with the band, seeing the audience. So you get a picture of that, and you write it.

With his new band and new sound, Brown was poised for a musical breakthrough. The breakthrough would have to wait, however, until Brown and his two recording labels could find common ground.

Besides pushing his music into new directions, Brown slowly became interested in the civil rights movement during the mid-1960s. During the 1950s, a number of events began to unfold as African Americans demanded better treatment: for too long, blacks had been treated as second-class citizens. In 1954, the United States Supreme Court ruled in *Brown v. Board of Education* that public school could no longer operate under the separate but equal doctrine. The following year, African Americans initiated a boycott against the segregated public bus system in Montgomery, Alabama, and a young minister named Martin Luther King Jr. rose to prominence. Following the boycott, the momentum for the movement grew, with whites and blacks marching and protesting for equal rights for African Americans throughout the South.

Martin Luther King Jr., accompanied by Lonnie King, (*left*), and an unidentified woman, walks by a segregation protester following his October 9, 1960, arrest in Atlanta.

Brown and his band were usually away from their Southern home, traveling on the road, and, for the most part, had little awareness of the growing civil rights movement. On the road, many hotels and restaurants were off limits to African Americans, but Brown and the band understood these rules, even if they did not like them: these were the same rules they had grown up with in Georgia. There were incidents, however, that made Brown at least partially aware that change was in the air.

On one occasion in 1961, Brown and several band members decided to eat at a local Trailways bus station in Birmingham, Alabama. Frequently, the band ate at bus stations in the South, because bus stations included "white" and "colored" sections in the dining room. Since the racial division was clear, the band could be sure to get a good meal without the possibility of trouble. As Brown and the others sat down and began eating, they heard a growing noise from the "white" section of the room. A number of blacks were waiting in line, perhaps college students: they intended to sit on the white side of the restaurant. When one of the seats was vacated, a young black man sat at the lunch counter next to a white man. After insulting the black man, the white man knocked the young black man off of the stool and onto the floor. Other young blacks came to take his place, and soon the restaurant erupted with whites assaulting blacks.

Brown and the band left in a hurry, found their parked car, and started to leave. Behind them, a bus started honking, signaling for Brown and the Flames to get out of the way. When the band moved its car out the way, however, they understood why the bus was in a hurry: the bus, carrying a number of black protesters, was being followed by carloads of angry whites carrying an assortment of weapons. Now the car that Brown and the Flames was driving was squeezed in-between the bus and the angry mob. As soon as they had their chance, they sped away. Later, they learned the bus was part of the Freedom Rider movement, a group of people who were challenging segregation in public transportation.

Even though Brown expressed little interest in the civil rights movement during the mid-1960s, he nonetheless drew a line when it came to playing segregated shows. At the end of 1964, he was scheduled to perform at the Bell Auditorium in Augusta, Georgia. Because of the terms of his parole after prison, Brown had not been allowed to return to his hometown for a number of years. With his parole completed, he returned to Augusta a local hero, the small town boy who made it big. Soon, however, his homecoming was spoiled: The Bell Auditorium planned to segregate Brown's show.

Freedom Riders sit on the roadside as their bus goes up in flames.

Brown was unhappy, but it seemed that little could be done. White people sat on one side of the theater, blacks on the other. A few days later, however, he performed in Macon, Georgia and discovered the same problem. Brown, however, was determined to force the issue this time. "I had just been through all that in Augusta and I wasn't going to go through it again, not in my second hometown."

Brown told his manager, Clint Brantley, that unless a change could be made, he would not perform. Brantley explained that the tickets had already been sold, and that it was doubtful, at this point, that anything could be done. Brown still insisted. Perhaps making whites and blacks sit in different places in the theater seemed normal in Macon, but it was not right.

Eventually, a solution was found. Instead of placing one group in the balcony and the other on the main floor, the balcony was closed off. Everyone, blacks and whites, was escorted on to the main floor of the theater, and when that section was filled up, more blacks and whites were escorted into the balcony section. There were no complaints or incidents: the show went as planned. When Brown returned to Augusta several months later, the same idea was used for the Bell Auditorium. Many community members in both Macon and Augusta had been surprised: they believed that non-segregated performances would lead to conflicts between whites and blacks. Instead, everyone was focused on the main event: a James Brown show.

After nearly a year of legal conflict, Brown resolved his differences with Nathan and King at the beginning of 1965. Nathan agreed to draw-up a new contract, one that offered Brown a better royalty rate on his recordings, and also promised $1,500 a week, no matter how well his recordings were doing on the charts. For Brown, the new contract gave him more power, which gave him more control over his career. Still, the victory was about more than power: a weekly check and better royalty rate were also about respect.

Brown had smoothed the road to reconciliation with a pre-deal gift to Nathan: before negotiations, he recorded a new song that continued the experiments of "Out of Sight." It was called "Papa's Got a Brand New Bag," and Brown and his new band members recorded it hastily in a studio in Charlotte, North Carolina. Brown remembered the recording:

> While recording "Papa's Got a Brand New Bag," I could feel something new kicking around inside me. Soon enough, I gave birth to a little baby I named funk, a gift delivered by Papa that was to become everybody's brand new bag! I had created something new and important for both Black and White audiences, and like the great Mr. Sinatra, I'm not ashamed to say I did it my way!

Brown wanted the song to have the same kind of energy as his live shows, so it was recorded live in the studio with no overdubs. The lyrics to the song were so new that Brown held the lyric sheet in his hand during the recording session. When the players gathered to listen to the first take, a number of people, including Brown, began dancing. Brown's manager, who paid for the session, informed everyone that the first take was good enough. The recording was delivered to Nathan, a peace offering, indicating that Brown was ready to return.

"Papa's Got a Brand New Bag" solidified an evolution in Brown's musical direction that had begun a year earlier with "Out of Sight." On one level, his music was more popular than ever. "Papa's Got a Brand New Bag" rose to number one on the R&B chart, and number eight on the *Billboard* Hot 100. On another level, it signaled to Brown's listeners that a new phase had been started in his career. Brown later remembered this career-defining moment:

James Brown performing on *Soul Train*, a popular music variety show. Funk ushered in a new, innovative, and upbeat sound. "I had discovered that my strength was not in the horns, it was in the rhythm," Brown wrote in his autobiography. "I was hearing everything, even the guitars, like they were drums." He also attributed the new musical style to what he called the "One." "The 'One' is derived from the Earth itself, the soil, the pine trees of my youth," Brown later said. "And most important,

it's on the upbeat—ONE two THREE four—not the downbeat, one TWO three FOUR, that most blues are written. Hey, I know what I'm talking about! I was born to the downbeat, and I can tell you without question there is not pride in it. The upbeat is rich, the downbeat is poor. Stepping up proud only happens on the aggressive 'One,' not the passive Two, and never on the lowdownbeat. In the end, it's not about music—it's about life."

> Right away, I got a new bag going. I was tellin'
> 'em in so many ways, too. To the listeners I was
> saying, Papa's doing his thing, eating dinner with
> his family, dancing with his family, going to the
> ball game with his kids. To the musicians I was
> saying, here's a new bag. Here's a new direction.
> Here's one that represents the people, not just
> Mozart, Schubert, Beethoven, Bach, Strauss,
> or Mantovani.

As soul had grown out of R&B, funk now grew out of soul. Funk, as the new music would be called, combined the basic elements of R&B, soul, and jazz to create a raw, down-to-earth sound. The word funk was derived from stink, drawing a connection between the earthiness of body sweat and the muscular sound of the music. Funk simplified soul and R&B, reducing the number of chords and removing much of the melody. As funk evolved in the late 1960s, some songs relied on no more than one chord, allowing the band to lay down polyrhythm as a backdrop to free-form vocals. Especially in concert, a performer like Brown and his band could vamp or ad lib on a song's rhythm for extended periods of time. Because the songs were frequently open ended and very long, the record label issued fewer singles of Brown's new music. Promoting the album, as had been the case with *Live at the Apollo*, frequently became more important.

"Papa's Got a Brand New Bag" became the first of a long list of hits that Brown recorded during the mid-to-late-1960s. This time period became one of his most creative, with each new song building on the innovations of the previous one. In 1967, "Cold Sweat" picked up where "Papa's Got a Brand New Bag" had left off. Like the previous song, "Cold Sweat" raced up the charts, reaching number one on the R&B chart and number seven on the *Billboard* Hot 100. Songs like "Cold Sweat" also attracted another kind of fan: other musicians.

When these songs hit the radio in the mid-1960s, they were unlike anything else available. Brown's radical departure from traditional R&B and soul fascinated other musicians, but also puzzled them. "Cold Sweat," for instance, only included one chord change, and Brown's band members placed the greatest emphasis on the first beat in each musical measure. Even the bridge, where the one chord change took place, seemed to defy the logic of tradition. The groove, built around an unusual drum pattern and heavy bass line, became everything. Brown and his band turned musical tradition on its head.

By the mid-1960s Brown had overcome his problems at King Records and ignited a musical revolution. His rebirth and growth attracted a new fan base and earned him a new nickname: Soul Brother Number One. After years of struggle, Brown's drive, creativity, and ceaseless effort had produced both economic and artistic triumphs. Soul Brother Number One was now one of the biggest, most influential artists in the United States.

James Brown performs at a night rally held on the last day of the March Against Fear at Tugaloo University in 1966.

Chapter Five

FROM BOSTON TO VIETNAM

By 1965-66, James Brown was a well-known public figure. His music reached millions of listeners, and innovative releases like "I Feel Good" were influencing a new generation of musicians. While Brown continued to work hard and tour incessantly, his success had allowed him to leave the grind of the chitlin' circuit behind: now he headlined theaters and coliseums for a premium fee. Brown's music also continued to break down traditional barriers, reaching both white and black audiences in concert and on the music charts. As a popular performer and a creative musical force, Brown had achieved much of what he had set out to achieve ten years earlier.

While Brown had no intention of resting on his hard-won success, his popularity helped expand his public role as a popular entertainer. He began to envision that a popular entertainer like himself could be more than an entertainer. As a public figure, he could also inform and educate others, perhaps even influence peoples' political views. As Brown began contributing to the civil rights movement in the mid-1960s, he found it difficult to draw a line between his political views and his music. During the mid-to-late-1960s, the line became even more blurry, with Brown performing at civil rights events and with his music incorporating civil rights themes. James Brown, the political proponent and James Brown, the popular funk star, was one and the same person, especially after the release of his 1968 hit song, "Say It Loud (I'm Black and I'm Proud)," which became an anthem of the rising Black Power movement. "I clearly remember," Brown later recalled, "we were calling ourselves colored, and after the song, we were calling ourselves black."

Brown's previous interest in the civil rights movement had been primarily personal. While he had paid little attention to the national movement, he worked to end segregation at his concerts in the South. After meeting activist James Meredith in 1966, Brown began to consider the broader issues of the civil rights movement.

James Meredith was publicly known for his involvement in the civil rights movement. In 1962, he became the first black student to be admitted to the University of Mississippi. Meredith also worked to establish black voting rights. In June of 1966, he initiated the "March Against Fear," an event designed to convince African Americans to register to vote. Meredith planned to walk from Memphis, Tennessee, to Jackson, Mississippi, to promote his initiative. After only three miles, however, Meredith was shot in the back.

Following the shooting, Brown traveled to a Cincinnati hospital to meet Meredith for the first time. Brown liked Meredith, and was convinced from the visit that he needed to become more politically involved. "It was no longer going to be enough to change the music of a generation—I had to try to change people's way of thinking as well." Brown explained his new philosophy to music journalist Charlie Gillett:

James Meredith being escorted by U.S. Marshals into the University of Mississippi

If I can use my position to bring about better understanding, I should take advantage of the opportunity. I want people to respect other people, to see that all kinds of different people, yellow, black, are people! To see that there are all ways of living, and they can exist side by side. I hope I can help to bring people closer together.

One of the first causes that Brown embraced was the need for young people to remain in school. He knew from personal experience that without an education, it was difficult and perhaps impossible to achieve the American Dream. In 1966, Brown wrote "Don't Be a Drop-Out." For many listeners, this song introduced a new side of James Brown. The song tells the story of a man with a number of problems, all of which stem from his lack of education. While his better-educated friends work hard and get ahead, he remains non-prosperous; while his friends buy new clothes and support their families, he remains dissolute. Although Brown himself had achieved a great deal without an education, he knew that his lack of education had held him back. Furthermore, he knew that not everyone could become a successful entertainer like himself. An education would allow anyone who worked hard the opportunity to get ahead.

"Don't Be a Drop-Out" was released in October of 1966, and Brown delivered a copy of the newly pressed single to Vice President Hubert Humphrey. Brown began visiting schools and told students about his own background as a drop-out; he explained that without his talent, he would probably be working as a manual laborer. Brown also built a sketch into his concerts that re-emphasized the message of "Don't Be a Drop-Out." In the sketch, members of the band pretended to be students. Brown's long-time musical partner, Bobby Byrd, played the part of a drop-out, reading a book upside down. Eventually, he is convinced to return to school. In a similar way, Brown encouraged drop-outs to return to school and work toward a general education diploma (GED). For one tour, Brown initiated a scholarship program, offering $500 in aid for students attending local black colleges.

Other efforts by Brown focused more directly on civil rights for African Americans. In 1966, he became a lifetime member of the National Association for the Advancement of Colored People (NAACP). He also joined publicly, providing publicity for the organization. Brown traveled to Tugaloo College in Jackson, Mississippi, in the summer of 1966 to perform at a civil rights rally. Brown also remained in close contact with Vice President Humphrey and was named, along with boxer Muhammad Ali, as the co-chair of the Vice President's Youth Opportunity Program in 1967. As the co-chair, Brown helped distribute literature and badges for the Don't Be a Dropout program to radio disc jockeys throughout the United States. While Brown's commitment to black politics continued to grow throughout 1966-67, it would be pushed to a new level in 1968.

On April 4, 1968, Martin Luther King Jr. was assassinated at a public rally in Memphis, Tennessee. King, perhaps more than anyone else during the 1960s, was the best known and most admired civil rights leader. Even as violence escalated in the 1960s, from the inner city riots of Detroit and Los Angeles to the ongoing participation of American soldiers in Vietnam, King insisted that the movement remain peaceful and non-confrontational. Blacks, he believed, could win a place within American society by asserting their rights to equality without resorting to violence. King's death sent shockwaves throughout America, though none more powerful than the waves that reverberated through black neighborhoods.

Martin Luther King Jr.

Brown, like many others, was deeply saddened by the assassination of Martin Luther King Jr. "When a great man is killed for no reason and he happens to be your friend, you feel the loss twice over." King's nonviolent approach to civil rights appealed to Brown: the singer saw no reason that whites and blacks could not find common ground. Brown realized that in the aftermath of King's assassination, however, that strong emotions might lead to violence. This, Brown believed, was the very thing that King would not have wanted.

After Brown's initial reaction to King's death, he wondered what he could do to help calm the situation. He began talking to those around him, and soon decided to broadcast messages on his two radio stations: WJBE in Knoxville, Tennessee, and WEBB in Baltimore, Maryland. Brown made a personal appeal to listeners: honor what Dr. King had stood for by committing no acts of violence.

Demonstrators with signs, one reading "Let his death not be in vain," in front of the White House, after the assassination of Martin Luther King Jr. in April 1968

Brown was also scheduled to perform a concert in Boston. He believed that the concert should go on, despite the tragedy of King's death: the concert would serve to keep many people off the streets of Boston. When Brown arrived in Boston, however, he found that city officials were unsure whether or not to go forward with the concert.

Brown was met at the airport by Boston councilman Thomas Atkins, who explained the ongoing situation. The previous night, Boston had remained quiet, still in shock over the assassination. City officials were worried, however, that violence might break out the following night and the National Guard remained on alert. The mayor, Kevin White, initially argued that the concert should be canceled; instead of going out to attend a concert, thousands of people would remain at home. Others countered that canceling the concert would just create more problems: if fans showed up at the concert hall and learned that the concert had been cancelled, then there might be more trouble. Finally, a solution was offered: allow the concert to go on as planned, but televise it. Whether people attended the concert or remained at home watching the concert on television, they would not be on the street at night, potentially causing problems.

Brown wanted to help, but he was in a contractual bind. He had just taped a program for television in New York City, and his contract prohibited him from performing on another televised program within a specified area. Boston fell within that area. Unless the New York station released him from his contract, the concert could not be legally aired on television in Boston. Further complicating matters, Mayor White planned to cancel the concert if it could not be televised.

Brown's staff worked out the details in New York, quickly obtaining permission to perform on Boston television. Before going forward, however, the televised concert hit one more snag: money. When many fans learned that the concert would be televised, they went to the coliseum to ask for refunds. As a result, Brown would be playing to an only partially filled stadium, while performing on television for free. To make up for his losses, Brown asked the city of Boston to cover the gate. This simply meant paying for any empty coliseum seats, since the concert—under normal circumstances—would have sold out. Mayor White hesitated, worrying that using taxpayer money to pay a well-known entertainer would be unpopular with Boston voters. Eventually, however, Councilman Atkins convinced the mayor that paying Brown was the right thing to do. With legal permission granted and a monetary agreement reached, the concert would go forward and be shown on television.

A local disc jockey, Early Byrd on WILD, helped set up the arrangements. WGBH, the local public television station, agreed to broadcast the concert. Brown's show opened with an appeal from Mayor White to the city: "I'm here tonight, like all of you, to listen to James. But I'm also here to ask for your all [sic] help. I'm here to ask you to stay with me as your mayor, and make Dr. King's dreams a reality in Boston." Brown opened with a similar plea: any violence would dishonor King's memory. When Brown finished his set at two o'clock in the morning, the streets of Boston were empty; the network, hoping that the calm would remain until morning, decided to air the program a second time. Brown was pleased that he might have played a role in keeping the peace in Boston and he hoped that a similar calm would descend on all American cities. "James Brown always gave his all," music journalist Tom Vikers recalled. "But that night, there was an emotional edge to it. He seemed totally present, in the moment, and giving 110 percent."

While Brown's hope for peace worked in Boston, it was premature for many other American cities. The next morning he learned that violence had broken out in the nation's capital, Washington, DC. Authorities asked him to speak publicly, but when he arrived in the city, local leaders expressed hesitation: they worried that Brown might not send the right message to angry blacks within the city. If he said the wrong thing, then the violence could grow worse. Finally, Brown spoke at the Municipal Center in the city, once again reminding a television audience of Martin Luther King's legacy. Slowly, the violence subsided, and Washington, DC, returned to order.

Brown's interest in politics also extended to a deep concern for the Americans who were serving in Vietnam. He had heard that many black soldiers complained that the United Service Organization (USO) offered little entertainment designed for blacks serving in the war, and he wanted to fill the gap. Singer Marva Whitney, who later traveled with Brown's revue to Vietnam, said that black servicemen considered the entertainers sent by the USO "Oreo Cookies": entertainers who were black on the outside, but too closely associated with whites on the inside. Brown, like many, also realized that a large number of African Americans had been sent to fight for freedom in a foreign country, while black rights still remained limited in the United States. He believed that despite the shortcomings of American equality, that many black soldiers completed their service out of patriotism, not just because they were drafted; that many black soldiers, just like white soldiers, believed in what American stood for. Brown petitioned the U.S. government to travel to Vietnam, but the army was hesitant about accepting his offer. "I'd been trying for a long time to get the government to let me go over there. I offered to pay all my expenses. But for some reason they didn't want me to go. I don't know if they thought I would be too political."

While Vietnam was far away from the civil rights movement, racial tension remained high among American troops. A disproportionate number of poor African Americans had been drafted to fight in Vietnam, and even if many chose to fight out of patriotism as Brown believed, critics charged that it was unfair that blacks carry such a heavy burden. Part of the tension between white and black soldiers came from the clash of different cultural backgrounds. The tension also increased following Martin Luther King's assassination.

On military bases, this tension was sometimes expressed over different musical tastes: white Southern soldiers liked country music, while black soldiers often preferred soul music. In many army clubs, however, country music dominated the jukebox during popular hours, meaning that everyone who attended these clubs had to listen to country. Author Richard Ford related one racial outburst over music. A group of black soldiers were returning from the jungle when they noticed a Confederate flag hanging from one of the barracks. Inside, air-conditioning was blasting cool air on soldiers who were dancing to country music. The black soldiers chased the white soldiers from the barracks and destroyed the stereo equipment.

Despite Brown's concern over black servicemen, he made his broader entertainment mission clear: he was traveling to Vietnam to entertain all soldiers, white and black, who were serving a patriotic cause. "I went to perform for even a step beyond that—humanity! 'Cause I wanted to see us as a people being able to get along with people around the world."

Even before the tour began, Brown received a great deal of criticism from the black community and liberal press. To his critics, traveling to Vietnam was equal to supporting a war that many believed unjust by 1968. For his black critics, he was labeled an Uncle Tom, someone who worked with whites at the expense of his own people, black Americans.

When Brown attended a White House dinner with President Lyndon Johnson before leaving for Vietnam, the criticism against him accelerated.

Brown made his own patriotism clear at the time in a song called "America Is My Home." Brown speaks the lyrics instead of singing them, and the song has been cited as an influence on rap. In the song, Brown states his belief that America is still the best country in the world. Even though whites and blacks may not always get along, they can be counted on to join together against outside enemies. If a person works hard and obtains an education, he or she can get ahead in America.

James Brown performs for American soldiers in Vietnam.

A 1968 photo of Brown leaning on his private jet. In 1966, he had bought his own Learjet, and around this same time he also established a restaurant franchise and acquired several radio stations. A 1969 cover story in *Look* magazine showcased Brown and his business empire, posing the question on its cover, "Is he the most important black man in America?"

In "America Is My Home," Brown also speaks of starting life as a shoeshine boy, but now, after working hard as an entertainer, owning his own jet.

The trip to Vietnam also impacted Brown financially. Since there had been little warning before the approval of the tour, he had to cancel $100,000 worth of performance dates. Brown also cut the band's pay on the eve of the difficult trip. Initially, the entire Brown Revue traveled to Tokyo, Japan, and the plan was to take everyone to Saigon in South Vietnam. Eventually, however, the U.S. military believed that it would be too dangerous and only allowed six musicians plus Brown to complete the trip.

Despite the criticism, reduced finances, and the problem of temporarily losing most of his band, Brown persevered. In June of 1968, he traveled with Tim Drummond, Jimmy Nolen, Maceo Parker, Waymon Reed, Clyde Stubblefield, and Marva Whitney to Saigon in South Vietnam. Even though the U.S. military controlled Saigon at the time, the streets of the city remained dangerous to civilians; South Vietnamese soldiers continually changed allegiances, and North Vietnamese hit men worked within the city. "Flying into Saigon, you could see all the blown-up buildings and damage that had been done," Brown said.

In the Army's schedule, Brown and the revue would leave Saigon each morning, play three shows at an army base, and return to Saigon in the evening. Each day for a week, Brown and the band boarded a plane or, more often, a helicopter, and flew to a new base. One show was performed in the morning, a second show during the day, and a final show in the evening. When the final show was finished, the band would return to their hotel rooms in Saigon.

On one morning flight, Brown and the band climbed aboard an old plane that reminded one band member of the airplanes that were always found crashed in the jungle during Tarzan movies. The pilot reassured the passengers of the plane's reliability, but shortly thereafter, the plane spouted an oil leak and caught on fire. While the plane continued to fly, it landed haphazardly on the edge of the Tan Son Nhut airfield in a swamp. Marva Whitney remembered the flight: "The pilot said, 'Everybody get out! And I mean move it!' We're in the marshes, the door opens, no time for a ladder. Would someone give me a helping hand? Forget it! . . . It was every man for himself, including me! I had to jump from the plane." After escaping from the aircraft, the Vietcong—North Vietnamese soldiers—attacked the plane. While everyone escaped without injury, Vietnam was a dangerous place, even for visiting musicians.

While Brown specifically came to Vietnam to entertain American troops, he and the members of his band—six black and one white—re-emphasized a powerful political message: blacks and whites could work and even prosper together. Tim Drummond, the only white member of the group, had wanted to be included on the trip for that very reason.

On the last show of the trip, Brown and his revue performed before 40,000 troops at Bear Cat stadium. The stadium had been carved out of the ground, like the Hollywood Bowl, and tanks, pointing toward the stage, stood positioned around the perimeter. In the background, bombs were falling, and Brown remembers the temperature rising to 115 degrees. The mass of soldiers promised to protect the musicians from Charlie, a nickname for North Vietnamese soldiers. Brown and the band kept on playing, and after the show, visited with the soldiers until it was time to fly back to Saigon. Thinking back on the experience after he had returned to America, Brown counted his blessings. "The whole time in Vietnam there was always a chance we'd get shot down or mortared, but nothing I did was as hard as what our soldiers had to do."

James Brown performs on the *Jerry Lewis Show* in 1969. A master dancer, Brown performed every dance craze there was in the 1950s and '60s: the "camel walk," the "mashed potato," and the "popcorn." He invented several of his own, too.

Chapter Six

TRAGEDY, TAXES, AND DISCO

With constant touring, making new records, and a deepening commitment to politics, James Brown led a very busy life in the late 1960s. As the 1960s came to a close, however, his busy life became more chaotic. Whereas the music continued to play a central part in his day-to-day activities, he was besieged by the Internal Revenue Service (IRS), the Federal Communications Commission (FCC), legal difficulties, personal tragedy, and a major shift in musical fashions. Many of these problems followed Brown throughout the 1970s, leaving the singer demoralized and, at times, seemingly forgotten in the face of new musical trends.

Beginning in the late 1960s, Brown faced a growing tax problem. He knew that he did not fully understand how to file his taxes: Brown's music business, made up of income from live shows, record sales, and the ownership in radio stations, was complicated. He wrote Vice President Hubert Humphrey, President Lyndon Johnson, and Attorney General Ramsey Clark, asking for assistance; he also wrote Richard Kleindienst of the IRS, asking for assistance. No one responded. Later, Brown received a letter from the IRS. He had been playing basketball with his oldest son Teddy and stopped to open the letter. The IRS claimed that Brown owed $1,870,000 in back taxes around 1968-69. He laughed and continued playing basketball: it was obviously, he believed, a mistake. "I thought it was a misunderstanding that eventually would be cleared up," Brown wrote in his autobiography, "so I went on about my life."

Vice President Hubert H. Humphrey, accompanied by Brown, addresses five hundred youngsters in the Watts section of Los Angeles during the summer of 1968.

In one instance, a man entered Brown's office in New York City with no introduction. He simply asked if Brown knew Velma Brown (Brown's former wife). Brown found the intruder rude and threatened to throw him out. The man left, and Brown later discovered that he had been from the IRS.

Brown initially ignored his IRS problem. When he was told by the IRS that he had a tax problem, he was indignant: it was the IRS, Brown said, that had a tax problem. Since Brown had asked for help and received none, he could not be blamed for any discrepancies. His anger over what he considered government intrusion into his life, however, stretched far into his past. How could a government that had never educated a man have any legal right to a portion of his income? How could a government that had never given a man a chance take his hard-earned money? While Brown may have believed that his cause was a righteous one, his reasoning failed to convince the IRS or the legal system that he no longer owed taxes. Later in the 1970s, Brown wrote President Jimmy Carter about his tax problem:

> They sent me a letter one time for tax evasion, so I wrote a letter back to President Jimmy Carter, who I knew very well, and I said, "Mr. President, you've seen my work and you know what I do." And I said "You cannot charge a man with tax evasion unless there's intent. Since I don't have an education beyond the seventh grade, there's not enough knowledge for there to be intent."

While no immediate action was taken, Brown's tax problem would return with vengeance over the next several years and continue to plague him for the remainder of his life.

If Brown felt assaulted from without by the federal government, one tragedy overwhelmed his tax problems. On June 14, 1973, Brown received a phone call from WRDW, one of his radio stations, that his oldest son Teddy had been killed in a car accident in upstate New York. Teddy, along with two friends, had apparently been driving all night and the following morning, the driver had fallen asleep. When the car slid off the road, it hit an embankment, killing everyone in the car. Brown was devastated.

Brown contacted his airplane pilots, and instructed them to meet him at the airport for the trip: he would have to fly to New York to identify the body of his son. When Brown arrived, however, he was visibly shaken, and the officials would not allow him to view the body.

After his son's death, Brown was haunted by recent disagreements with Teddy. Teddy had his own musical group, Teddy Brown and the Torches, and wanted to be a performer. Brown believed that his son was talented, though lacking in drive. "He could sing and dance, and hold his own even against me," Brown later recalled. While he was proud of Teddy's ability as a performer, he wanted his son to go to college, to have the educational opportunities he never had. Teddy refused to continue with his school, however, and the father and son had quarreled over this issue. Further complicating the relationship, Teddy, like his father as a boy, was starting to get in trouble. He passed bad checks, and it seemed only a matter of time before he faced legal problems. Brown was saddened over their disagreements and saddened because all of Teddy's potential was lost.

Many people that worked for Brown were surprised when he did not cancel three shows that were scheduled at that time in Dayton and Columbus, Ohio, and Buffalo, New York. They believed he would be too despondent to perform. Brown, however, refused to cancel the shows: he needed to keep busy or else he felt like he would lose his mind. In retrospect he doubted that he gave his best performances at these shows, but felt they were part of the healing process. After losing his son, Brown would place even more emphasis on his new home life in Augusta, Georgia, with his second wife, Deidre "Dee Dee" Jenkins. He also befriended a nineteen-year-old aspiring black activist named Al Sharpton, who had come from

Brown with his wife Deidre

a broken home like him. "I became in effect, over the next decade, his surrogate son, and he was my surrogate father," said Sharpton, who eventually married one of Brown's singers.

Despite these problems, Brown attempted to move forward with his music. Even here, however, he was besieged by difficulties. In the late 1960s, a number of the musicians who had helped Brown create a musical revolution left him.

Even early in his career, Brown gained a reputation as someone who was difficult to work with in a band. His earliest bands had clashed over ego problems: Brown, his band mates often felt, had to be the center of attention. As a bandleader, he was also known as a difficult taskmaster, expecting nothing less than perfection from musicians, singers, and dancers. Brown wanted the biggest and best show in the music business and demanded professionalism from everyone who worked in his music revue. Everyone wore uniforms and everyone was expected to arrive at the auditorium in a timely manner for the show. Because Brown improvised during a show, everyone was expected to keep an eye on him. "I stand behind my regimen," Brown later explained. "We do everything we can to protect the musicians, but I'm a firm person and I will fire my daddy. My daddy was workin' for me one time, and he didn't show like he shoulda. I fired my father."

When a singer or musician failed to meet these exacting standards, Brown fined him or her. If a musician arrived late or did not properly shine his shoes, he was fined. If someone made a mistake during a show, Brown would signal—using his fingers—how much the person would be fined. These mistakes, he believed, reflected poorly on him and would not be tolerated. "I put in a system of fines—so much for a dirty uniform, for unshined shoes, for being late," Brown later wrote. "If someone showed up drunk, he sat out and might get fired. Some of the cats resented the fines, but I think it gave me the tightest band in show business."

In the spring of 1970, the relationship between Brown's band and the singer reached a breaking point. The band had just finished a tour in Africa, and many of the members believed they were being paid too little. In March the heart of Brown's band, Maceo and Melvin Parker, Jimmy Nolen, and "County" Kellum, quit. While Brown quickly replaced the band with an equally supportive group of players, including bassist Bootsy Collins, turnover continued to be a problem throughout the 1970s.

Brown's attempt to move forward with his music was also complicated when he changed record labels. In 1971, he moved from

King Records to Polydor. He had doubts about moving to the new label, but eventually went forward nonetheless. Even though he made a great deal more money than he had at King, he remained unhappy with Polydor: he believed the label sabotaged his music. The company signed him, he thought, to gain credibility in the American market: once they had signed a major star, the German company would have a foothold in the American music business. Once they had signed him Polydor had little interest in developing his career. As a large corporation, Polydor lacked the personal touch of King.

Brown's biggest complaint was Polydor's seeming inability to understand his music. While the company had better recording studios than King, the producers and engineers had no knowledge of what it took to make a good James Brown record. Brown's contract allowed for complete artistic freedom, much more than he had ever had at King, and he personally mixed and oversaw his new recordings. Despite this contractual freedom, Polydor frequently interfered in the studio and remixed Brown's recordings. He could be funky, but not too funky or he might risk losing his more mainstream market. Brown also accused the company of failing to understand how to promote his records. While Brown's success continued on the singles' charts throughout the 1970s, his music was often relegated to the R&B charts. His hits were also less frequent.

Whether Brown's musical problems were caused by Polydor or a creative decline, critics complained that Brown's music had become repetitive and, often, preachy. His music had changed very little from the funky grooves of his best tracks of the mid-1960s, and now seemed more focused on a social message than the music itself. Many also argued that the constant turnover in his bands was hurting the final musical product.

Brown's trademark funky grooves also suffered from a change in musical trends. During the early 1970s, a new music called disco bubbled up from the underground, focusing on a strong beat for dancing. Disco drew a great deal from earlier black performers like Brown and Sly Stone, and matured in both black and gay dance clubs in a number of American and European cities. By 1975 disco filtered into the mainstream, creating a major trend that would last through the remainder of the decade. The popularity of disco also eclipsed the music of other performers like Brown on the popularity charts. Brown, in the wake of a new trend, appeared old fashioned to many.

Brown compounded his musical problems by allowing Polydor to eventually bring in outside producers to work on new material in the studio during the late 1970s. An outside producer, the label felt, would give Brown a new start, an effort toward making him more relevant for the new era. With new producers in the studio, Brown cut two albums during the late 1970s, both emulating the current disco trend. "So they watered down my sound a little bit but only so's that hopefully all the people could see what it's all about and once they latch on we'll get back to the hard-core James Brown." Neither album, however, was well received. When albums like *The Original Disco Man* failed to catch on, Brown and Polydor severed their relations.

Brown recognized the new music as borrowing from funk but was critical of how it developed. Disco, he believed, always stayed on the surface of the groove, while funk dug into the groove. Disco also focused on the record producer and the disc jockey, not the artist. Anyone, in the studio, could put together an endless disco groove. The importance of records and disc jockeys also undercut live performers: in disco, the featured performance was the dancers themselves, not the musicians. The change in musical styles also impacted where and how often Brown worked as a performer.

Brown performing in Munich, Germany, in 1973.

THE GREATEST MUSIC FESTIVAL THAT YOU HAVE NEVER SEEN...

SOUL POWER

THE
SPINNERS   B.B.
KING   CELIA
CRUZ   BILL
WITHERS   MIRIAM
MAKEBA   THE
CRUSADERS   BIG
BLACK

A SONY PICTURES CLASSICS RELEASE DASFILMS, LTD. PRESENTS AN ANTIDOTE FILMS PRODUCTION OF A FILM BY JEFFREY LEVY-HINTE "SOUL POWER" JAMES BROWN AND THE J.B.'s MUHAMMAD ALI THE SPINNERS B.B. KING BILL WITHERS CELIA CRUZ AND THE FANIA ALL-STARS FRANCO TABU LEY BIG BLACK THE CRUSADERS DON KING STEWART LEVINE LLOYD PRICE CINEMATOGRAPHY BY PAUL GOLDSMITH ALBERT MAYSLES RODERICK YOUNG EDITED BY DAVID SMITH MUSIC FESTIVAL PRODUCERS HUGH MASEKELA STEWART LEVINE ORIGINALLY CONCEIVED BY STEWART LEVINE PRODUCED BY DAVID SONENBERG
PRODUCED AND DIRECTED BY JEFFREY LEVY-HINTE
SONY PICTURE

PG-13 PARENTS STRONGLY CAUTIONED
Some Material May Be Inappropriate for Children Under 13
FOR SOME THEMATIC ELEMENTS AND BRIEF STRONG LANGUAGE
A
WWW.SOULPOWERFILM.COM WWW.SONYCLASSICS.COM
© 2009 DASFILMS LTD / ANTIDOTE INTERNATIONAL FILMS, INC. ALL RIGHTS RESERVED.
©2009 SONY PICTURES ENTERTAINMENT

Despite these shifts in musical taste, and despite Brown's waning popularity, he continued to place many singles on *Billboard* charts. In 1971, "Soul Power" reached number three on the R&B chart, and number twenty-two on the Hot 100; the following year Brown returned with "King Heroin," which reached number six on the R&B chart and number forty on the Hot 100. Two soundtrack albums, *Black Caesar* and *Slaughter's Big Rip-Off,* appeared on both the R&B album chart and the *Billboard* 200 in 1973; and *The Payback* reached number one on the R&B album chart while the single "The Payback" reached number one on the R&B singles chart in 1974. Other singles, "Funky President (People It's Bad)" in 1975, "Get Up Offa That Thing" in 1976, and "It's Too Funky in Here" in 1979 also reached the singles charts.

While the 1970s were difficult years for Brown, he nonetheless celebrated a number of triumphs. One of the highlights of these years was a trip to Kinshasa, Zaire, (now known as The Democratic Republic of the Congo) in 1974 to headline a three-day music festival. The festival was created by South African singer and composer Hugh Masekela and Stewart Levine to compliment what was being called the "Rumble in the Jungle," the heavyweight title fight between George Foreman and Muhammad Ali.

The promoters of the festival had a simple idea: they would bring the best African American talent from the United States to the homeland, Africa, and showcase that talent for the world. "I had a desire to hip the general audience to what wasn't yet called world music," Levine later recalled. "And I had this cockamamie idea about the festival, and everybody said yeah." Brown was joined by many other American performers, including blues guitarist/singer B. B. King, the pop-soul group the Spinners, and singer Bill Withers. These American performers were joined by Miriam Makeba of South Africa and Zairean's Tabu Ley Rochereau. As Brown said of the moment, "I just feel I'm a part of a great movement."

Poster promoting the documentary film *Soul Power,* the live music festival that accompanied the "Rumble in the Jungle" heavyweight boxing championship match between Muhammad Ali and George Foreman in Zaire, in 1974.

The task of mounting a three-day festival was extraordinarily involved, but the enthusiasm of the performers and promoters pushed the project forward. Initial problems included loading the plane with all the musicians and all of the musicians' equipment in New York City. As the plane was being loaded, Brown and his revue arrived, carrying 40,000 pounds worth of extra equipment. A sound system had been designed for the stage in Zaire, but Brown insisted on carrying his own sound equipment. Furthermore, the equipment was too heavy for the plane, but Brown refused to come along without it. The equipment was eventually loaded and the flight proceeded, but not without a near mishap after stopping for fuel in Madrid. "We touched the trees in Madrid on the runway," Levine recalled. "That's how severely overweight the plane was."

While some considered Brown's actions humorous in retrospect, others were bothered by his demands. "His actions were suicidal," poet Quincy Troupe recalled of the trip. "But James Brown's attitude, from the beginning, was insane. Some of it being show biz, part of the mask that's expected of you, but James Brown went beyond that. It was incredible. I had to admire the flight velocity of his ego."

James Brown's performance at the festival was captured by documentary filmmaker Albert Maysles, but the footage— because of lack of funds—remained stored in the vaults for many years. Eventually, the footage would be assembled into *Soul Power* in 2008, and the highlight of the film is Brown's concert. As he takes the stage, Brown, wearing a pantsuit with an embroidered G.F.O.S. (God Father of Soul), dances, performs a split, and moves his feet to one of his newer hits in 1974, "The Payback." The stage is filled with singers, dancers, drummers, and a large horn section. Brown humorously tells the audience that he does not like to perform the best of James Brown because, "the best of James Brown is yet to come." He also performed "Cold Sweat" at the festival and in celebration of an event featuring black talent, sang "Say It Loud—and I'm Proud."

Following the death of his son, problems with the IRS, and other multiple career difficulties, Brown's personal and performance life seemed to suffer setbacks for the remainder of the 1970s. After losing his second airplane due to tax problems, Brown's ability to perform was severely curtailed. Because the plane had allowed him to save extra time when traveling to concerts, he was able to remain at home more often and address a number of business matters between shows. By saving time and resting between shows, he was also able to schedule more shows and maintain a higher performance level. Now, he was back to traveling by car or commercial flights, just as he had been in his earlier days as a performer. These difficulties also lessened his ability to make money.

Eventually Brown's problems spilled over into his home life. His wife, "Dee Dee" Jenkins Brown, had traveled with him during the beginning of their relationship, but over time, she wanted Brown, herself, and their two daughters to have a home life. Brown agreed. He felt guilty over the effect of a broken home on his first son, Teddy, and wanted to spend more time with his new family. Following his problems with the IRS and the loss of his plane, however, Brown began to stay away from home once again. His wife also knew that the more time Brown spent away from home, the more likely he would befriend other women on the road. Eventually, Jenkins left Brown, and in the early 1980s, they divorced.

By the end of the decade, Brown was nearly broke, alone, and demoralized. Early in the decade, he had seemingly lost the heart of his white audience: now, he was seemingly in the process of also losing his black audience. His music seemed out-of-date, and when he tried to work within the restraints of disco, the results were unspectacular. After nearly twenty-five years in the music business, James Brown, the man with endless energy, ideas, and ambition, seemed ready to give up.

St. John the Baptist Parish Library
2920 New Hwy. 51
LaPlace, LA 70068

Brown in 1999 at the Woodstock 99 concert at Gri ss Air Force Base in Rome, New York

Chapter Seven

HOME TO GEORGIA

By the end of the 1970s, Brown's musical career was in shambles. His recordings reached fewer and fewer listeners, and, by 1981, his contract with Polydor came to an end. With the rise and popularity of disco and New Wave, Brown found himself out of public favor, leaving him fewer opportunities to perform live. Critics also expressed less interest in his music, arguing that the best days of Brown as a recording artist were behind him. On occasion, his erratic behavior also created clashes. Scheduled to perform at Madison Square Garden with the Rolling Stones in 1981, Brown canceled when promoter Bill Graham refused to transport the singer and his band from Augusta, Georgia, to the stadium. Frequent turnover in band personnel and an attempt to copy the popular style of the day (disco) further damaged Brown's credibility.

Brown's personal life was equally in disorder. By January 1981, his eleven-year marriage to Deidre Brown came to an end. The divorce also ended Brown's dream of providing the kind of home life for his two daughters that he had not provided for his first son, Teddy. Besides family problems, Brown remained under pressure from the IRS, depriving him of his home in Augusta, Georgia, and leaving him nearly broke. For many, Brown had become yesterday's celebrity—old news, and someone who was no longer taken seriously.

During the early 1980s, comedian Eddie Murphy parodied Brown in a sketch for *Saturday Night Live*, titled "Celebrity Hot Tub Party." Wearing big hair and a robe, Murphy sang a song called "Hot Tub," emitting Brown's trademark squall as he stuck his foot in the hot tub that had been placed in the middle of the stage. The comedian's backing band emulated Brown's late 1960s funk, and when Murphy complained of sweating, the musicians pretended to fan the overheated singer. Murphy even mimics Brown's trademark cape routine during the sketch. While Brown was not the only musician that Murphy lampooned (he also satirized Stevie Wonder), this sketch re-enforced criticism of Brown dating back to the late 1960s: Brown, as a musician and a performer, had become a parody of himself; his music no longer evolved and the endless vamps of his stage act had become clichés. Murphy's sketch simply summed up what had become—to many—conventional wisdom on Brown.

Even by the time of Murphy's sketch on *Saturday Night Live*, however, Brown was staging a comeback. Furthermore, his musical legacy received a boost when disco was pushed aside by a new music that drew heavily from Brown's classic work: rap. Sampling Brown's earlier work offered new rap artists a solid base of funk to launch their lyrical street poetry.

The first incident that marked Brown's resurgence was put in motion by two other comedians who had made their reputations on *Saturday Night Live*. One night, while Brown was performing at the Lone Star in Greenwich Village, Dan Aykroyd and John Belushi watched his show. Both were initially known for their work on *Saturday Night Live*, but now were appearing in movies.

Brown accumulated many titles during his career: "The Hardest-Working Man in Show Business," "Soul Brother Number One," "The Godfather of Soul," "The Minister of New New Super Heavy Funk," "Mr. Dynamite," "Mr. Please Please Please," "The Boss," and the best known, "Godfather of Soul."

They were scheduled to star in a new movie directed by John Landis, based on two characters, Jake and Elwood, who sang blues songs on *Saturday Night Live*. The movie would simply be called *The Blues Brothers*, and Aykroyd and Belushi thought that Brown would be perfect for the part of the minister in the movie. Aykroyd and Belushi contacted Brown through his agent, Richard Dostel.

At first, Brown hesitated to read the script: African American culture played a significant part in the movie, and he worried that the script might portray black culture negatively. Eventually, Brown was won over, believing that the movie explored black music history from the blues to R&B in a thoughtful manner. After deciding to accept the role, Brown also realized that he was born to play the part of a black minister, the Reverend Cleophus James. He had sung gospel in church as a boy, and he had sung gospel in the Ever Ready Gospel Singers and Gospel Starlighters during the early 1950s. As familiar as he was with gospel music, however, Brown found it funny that Landis asked him to sing a gospel song with which he was unfamiliar, "The Old Landmark."

Brown memorized his lines on his flight to California. The movie would be filmed on Universal Studios' lot where a reproduction of a Chicago church had been built. Once he arrived, Brown also discussed his role with Landis. At a certain point in his scene, for instance, Brown was supposed to remove his minister's robe. In a fashion, removing the robe would have referred to Brown's stage routine, where a robe or cape was placed on his shoulders and then discarded. Since he was playing a role and not himself, Brown convinced Landis to drop that part of the scene. It would take three days to shoot Brown's scene.

In Brown's scene as the Reverend Cleophus James in *The Blues Brothers*, he leads a large, lively group of church attendees in "The Old Landmark." He is backed by a choir and a band, and the church members clap and sing along. A number of church members, dressed in colorful clothing, dance in the aisles. As Brown and the others perform, Jake and Elwood watch from the back of the church. Suddenly, a light from the sun breaks through the church and shines on Elwood, turning him blue. Brown's minister shouts out, "Do you see the light?" Elwood, answering affirmatively, begins to turn cartwheels up the church aisle, and soon, both brothers are dancing to the music.

The Blues Brothers was released in June of 1980 and became a popular summer film. While Brown's part in the film was no

Brown as Reverend Cleophus
James in *The Blues Brothers*

more than a cameo, it reminded music lovers of two things: of Brown's rich legacy that dated back to gospel and early R&B, and that Brown, now in his late forties, still was a powerful singer and performer. Soon, new opportunities were pouring in for Brown.

In November, Brown made three appearances at a number of Keystone Clubs owned by Bobby Corona and Freddie Herrera in the San Francisco area. Once again, Brown put together a large revue of fourteen musicians and singers, and the shows drew an estimated 6,000 people. He also performed a show at San Quentin, a prison in California. Each of Brown's shows opened with the J. B.'s International, Brown's back-up band, offering instrumental versions of the *Star Wars* theme and "We Are Funky Men." After the J. B.s warmed up the crowd, Brown appeared on stage for a seventy-five minute workout, though his last show of the evening typically lasted more than two hours. This was the first time Brown had performed in San Francisco in twelve years.

On December 13, 1980, Brown appeared on *Saturday Night Live*, once again, introducing himself to a younger audience that was unfamiliar with his earlier musical accomplishments. From the end of 1980 through 1981, Brown also taped a show with talk show host Tom Snyder, appeared on an hour program on Ted Turner's television station in Atlanta, Georgia, and performed at halftime during the Super Bowl. Dan Aykroyd asked him to appear in *Doctor Detroit*, and Brown's sequence was filmed at the end of 1982.

While Brown's appearance in *The Blues Brothers* had helped place him back in the public eye, a song connected to another movie completed his comeback. In 1985, he was offered another part in *Rocky IV* and a new song to sing, "Living in America." Brown hesitated at first, worrying that four Rocky movies were too many. After speaking with the movie's star, Sylvester Stallone, however, he changed his mind. Stallone spoke of his movies and how he hoped to set an example about the importance of values to younger viewers. Stallone also worried about the influence of violence on children from other movies he had made, like *Rambo*. Convinced of his good intentions, Brown accepted the part.

"Living in America" was written by Dan Hartman and Charlie Midnight, and was included on the *Rocky IV* soundtrack and issued as a single. The song rose to number four on the *Billboard* 100 at the beginning of 1986, becoming Brown's highest-charting single ever. While Brown had not written the song, he believed the song captured his life on the road. The song's portrait of traveling the American highway, moving from one city to the next, eating and drinking coffee in diners, was the life Brown had led since the early 1950s. "Living in America" also seemed to echo early Brown songs like, "America Is My Home," and offered a new way for the singer to express his patriotism and belief in the American Dream. Brown's climb from poverty in Augusta, Georgia, to a wealthy entertainer known around the world was proof that anyone, with talent and drive, could become somebody in America.

Brown's newfound success, however, was short-lived. Soon, many of the troubles that had besieged him during the 1970s returned in full force. During the summer, he was in a car accident, and later in the year, he received a ticket for reckless driving; eventually he was arrested after another traffic violation. Many within Brown's inner group noted his erratic behavior, and rumors circulated about spousal and drug abuse. These incidents, however, were only a prelude of what was to come.

Over a two-year period of time, the police were summoned to Brown's home ten times. Two of those calls were for domestic violence. In 1982, Brown had met his third wife, Adrienne Rodriguez, a makeup artist. "His wife would call and tell us he's beating her," noted James W. Whitehurst of the Aiken County Sheriff's Department. "He was shooting at her. She was shooting at him. One time he shot her mink coat full of holes. We were concerned the situation could develop into a homicide."

On April 3, 1988, the police were called to Brown's home for a domestic dispute, leading to an assault and battery charge against the singer. Brown's wife filed for divorce the same month, citing that he had mistreated her, "over the years by slapping her

Brown and his third wife, Adrienne

around, throwing things at her, shooting at her, knocked her teeth out . . . and on April 3, 1988 cut up her clothes, beat her with his fist and an iron pipe, inflicting various injuries requiring hospital treatment." There were also charges of drug possession by Brown. Following one arrest, police located a nasal spray bottle that contained PCP, a psychedelic drug sometimes referred to as angel dust.

All of these incidents climaxed at the end of September in 1988. On September 24, Brown burst into an office building carrying a shotgun. From Brown's point of view, later revealed in an FBI file, he had simply driven to his office at the Top Notch building near Augusta, Georgia. When he arrived, he found the bathroom door open and believed that someone had broken into his office. He returned to his truck and brought his shotgun back into the office. Soon, however, Brown learned that there was a meeting in another office in the complex. He came into the room where businesswoman Geraldine Phillips was holding an insurance seminar, laid his shotgun in the corner, and questioned everyone about using his office restroom. He then asked for the keys to the restroom, which he received, and then he locked the restroom.

The incident, however, was only a prelude to a police car chase. When Brown left the facility, he got into his truck and began driving on Interstate 20. When he noticed two police cars forming a roadblock, he drove around them, believing that they were attempting to apprehend someone else. Soon, however, the police officers pulled Brown over. Six other police cars arrived on the scene, and one of the police officers, Brown testified, kicked his car and broke his car window out with the barrel of a gun. Brown then reported to the FBI that the police shot at the hood and tires of his car and Brown, fearing for his life, drove away even though his tires were flat. Once the police caught him, he accused them of using unnecessary force, including a blow to the face that damaged his denture implant.

Brown's account, however, was challenged by others. Phillips found Brown's behavior less than rational. "He had grass in his hair," she said. "He said rats and roaches were running out of his hat." She said that Brown asked a number of nonsensical questions and that she was afraid that if she answered them wrong, Brown would kill everyone in the room. One person in the room quietly left and called the police. Phillips remembered that when the sirens became audible, Brown left.

The police likewise disputed Brown's testimony of the incident and viewed Brown as dangerous. While trying to stop Brown at an intersection, two officers said that he tried to run over them. As a result, they fired seventeen rounds, hitting two of Brown's tires. Following the gunfire, Brown led the police on a chase, driving as fast as eighty miles per hour. Eventually, Brown drove across the Georgia border into South Carolina, and the South Carolina police continued the chase. By the time Brown had reached the home of a friend in Augusta, he was being followed by fourteen police cars. The police officers arrested Brown. "Ironically," Brown later wrote, "I landed in a ditch about a mile from where I had first been arrested as a boy."

After his arrest, Brown quickly made bond, securing a temporary release. The following morning, however, he was arrested while driving his Lincoln Town Car under the influence of PCP, a hallucinogenic drug. Many believed that both Brown and his wife were misusing PCP, and that drug accounted for Brown's erratic behavior. Writer Amy Linden, who interviewed Brown, noted the drug's effects:

> PCP was such a weird drug for someone that age to start doing. It's like giving yourself a nervous breakdown. I've never met anyone who was sane who did it. It's not a young person's drug, it's not even a black drug; it's a white or Latino street drug. It's weird that he [Brown] would choose something that has no good side to it. You just get out there on it.

Brown was sentenced on December 17, 1988, in an Aiken, South Carolina, courtroom to six years in prison. Because his crimes occurred in two states, he had a second trial in Augusta, Georgia, for a series of charges including carrying a deadly weapon, driving under the influence, and assault. At the second trial, Brown received a concurrent six-year sentence, meaning that it was possible for Brown to serve twelve years in prison, depending on whether his behavior was good. While Brown disputed most of the accusations against him, he did not necessarily resent his prison sentence. "I wasn't arrested—I was rescued," Brown later wrote. "I was into some bad things and in need of help. I call my time in prison the poor man's Medicare!"

Brown's mug shot

Brown continued to maintain that he was innocent and that he was being persecuted by the police because he was a successful black man.

After a twenty-six month prison sentence, Brown experienced more legal problems and turmoil in his personal life. He continued his relationship with Adrienne Brown and stated publicly that the couple had become closer during his incarceration. Still, there would be another charge of spousal abuse at the end of 1994. In 1996, Adrienne Brown overdosed on prescription drugs and, after a brief hospitalization, recovered. On January 4, 1996, forty-five-year-old Adrienne Brown underwent eight hours of liposuction surgery. Two days later, resting in a recovery facility, she died. An autopsy revealed that a reaction to both legal and illegal drugs, combined with a weakened physical system following surgery, had killed her. James Brown was devastated with the loss, recalling—at the time—the loss of his son Teddy nearly twenty years earlier.

Brown at the Kennedy Center Honors
on December 7, 2003

Despite the multiple problems that surrounded Brown following his release from prison in 1991, he worked hard to rebuild his career. He continued to tour and made appearances at the American Music Awards and the Grammys in 1992. In 1995, Brown toured Europe during the summer and performed in Cleveland at the opening of the Rock and Roll Hall of Fame. In 1997, he received a star on the Hollywood Walk of Fame and was one of the featured performers at Super Bowl halftime. In the summer of 2000, Brown was inducted into the Songwriters Hall of Fame. He also received wide recognition for his contribution to black music from many rappers: Brown would become the recording artist most sampled. In 2001, Brown welcomed a new son and named him James Joseph Brown II. Brown's companion, Tomi Rae Hynie, gave birth to their son on June 11.

One of Brown's proudest achievements came on December 7, 2003. It was gala week at the Kennedy Center in Washington, DC, with the institution awarding American entertainers lifetime achievement awards. To Brown, the lifetime award meant more than public recognition for his more than forty years of musical creativity and more than a tribute to his ability as a performer. Instead, the award came down to one thing: respect. The very fact that a prestigious institution like the Kennedy Center chose Brown, a black man who had grown up poor in a small town in Georgia, said something about America.

Brown always maintained that anyone who put forth the effort could succeed in America, and he was living proof of that. As Brown accepted the award, he was known throughout the United States and throughout the world; Brown's music was listened to by whites, blacks, Latinos, and many other ethnic groups. Even with the social disadvantage of growing up within Southern society during segregation, even with the disadvantage of little education, Brown had fulfilled the American Dream.

On December 23, 2006, Brown arrived late for an appointment for dental implants. Noticing that Brown seemed confused and that he looked unhealthy, his dentist recommended

that he seek medical care. Brown checked himself into the Emory Crawford Long Memorial Hospital in Atlanta, Georgia, the following day. His manager later noted that Brown had been suffering from a cough since returning from Europe in November. As was typical of Brown, however, he did not talk about feeling unwell or seek medical attention.

While in the hospital, Brown canceled shows in Waterbury, Connecticut, and Englewood, New Jersey. He expressed his belief, however, that he would be ready to perform at several New Year's Eve celebrations, including appearing on newscaster Anderson Cooper's special on CNN. Despite his confidence, his health grew worse, and at 1:45 a.m. on December 25, James Brown died.

A public memorial service was held on December 28 at the Apollo Theater in Harlem, the very place where the "Godfather of Soul" and icon of African-American pride had recorded the legendary album, *Live at the Apollo,* more than forty years earlier. At the service, Brown's body was placed in a gold plated casket

Bruno Mars

encased by a glass box, which was carried by a horse-drawn carriage through the streets of New York City. Services were also held at the James Brown Arena in Augusta, Georgia, and in North Augusta. The Reverend Al Sharpton officiated. Many of the services displayed the same flare that had marked Brown's life—one even turned into a concert, with singing, handclapping, and dancing. At the end of it all, Brown's famous cape was laid upon his casket, just as it was laid across his shoulders and back so many times during his concerts.

Brown with will.i.am of the Black Eyed Peas and Justin Timberlake in 2005

The Godfather of Soul with the King of Pop, Michael Jackson, in 2003

Usher performing a duet with Brown in 2005

James Brown inspired a generation of entertainers like Mick Jagger, Prince, Public Enemy, and Usher. His music is the bedrock of hip-hop—more than one thousand songs use samples from Brown's seventy-eight albums. The late Michael Jackson called Brown "my greatest inspiration" and singer-songwriter Bruno Mars, who often wears a '50s pompadour and channels Brown when he dances, says watching the Godfather of Soul "changed my life."

TIMELINE

1933 Born James Joseph Brown, Jr. on May 3, in Barnwell, South Carolina.

1937 Mother, Susan Brown, leaves the family.

1949 Sentenced to eight to sixteen years in prison for breaking and entering; sent to the Alto Reform School outside of Toccoa, Georgia; in prison receives the nickname Music Box.

1952 Paroled early for good behavior; moves to Toccoa and befriends a local singer named Bobby Byrd; helps form the Ever Ready Gospel Singers; the Ever Ready Gospel Singers record a demonstration record of "His Eye Is on the Sparrow."

1953 Along with Bobby Byrd, transforms the Gospel Starlighters into the Avons, switching from gospel music to rhythm and blues.

1955 The Avons are renamed the Flames and then the Famous Flames; Clint Brantley, singer Little Richard's manager, also agrees to manage the Famous Flames.

1956 Ralph Bass signs the Famous Flames to King Records of Cincinnati; the Famous Flames record "Please, Please, Please"; "Please, Please, Please" reaches number five on the *Billboard* R&B chart.

1957 Forms a new version of the Flames after the original version of the Famous Flames breaks up.

1959 Performs his first show at the influential Harlem entertainment center, the Apollo Theater, appearing with Little Willie John; reunites with his mother after twenty years.

1961   Appears on Dick Clark's *American Bandstand*.

1962   Records four shows on October 24 at the Apollo Theater in Harlem; the edited tapes will become *Live at the Apollo*.

1963   King Records issues *Live at the Apollo*, which reaches number two on the *Billboard* 200 album chart.

1964   Attempts to leave King for Smash Records; legal proceedings by both labels, however, place his recording career on hold for nearly one year; appears in a Frankie Avalon movie, *Ski Party*.

1965   Returns to King Records and releases "Papa's Got a Brand New Bag"; "Papa's Got a Brand New Bag" climbs to number one on *Billboard*'s R&B chart and number eight on the Hot 100.

1966   Releases "Don't Be a Drop-Out" and begins working with Vice President Hubert H. Humphrey on a program to keep students in school; joins the National Association for the Advancement of Colored People (NAACP).

1967   Appears for the first time on *The Tonight Show* with Johnny Carson; appointed co-chair of Vice President Humphrey's Youth Opportunity Program; "Cold Sweat" rises to number one on the *Billboard* R&B chart and number seven on the Hot 100.

1968   Purchases WJBE in Knoxville; appears on public television in Boston after the assassination of Martin Luther King Jr.; tours Vietnam, performing for American soldiers.

1970   Marries Deidre Yvonne Jenkins.

1971   Signs with Polydor Records.

1972   Records the soundtrack for the film *Black Caesar*.

1973 First son, Teddy, killed in an automobile accident in New York State.

1974 Performs at the heavyweight title fight between Muhammad Ali and George Foreman in Kinshasa, Zaire.

1979 Becomes the first R&B artist to perform at the Grand Ole Opry in Nashville, Tennessee; loses his home in Augusta after continued tax problems.

1980 Appears in a cameo as a singing preacher in *The Blues Brothers*, a movie starring John Belushi and Dan Aykroyd; performs on *Saturday Night Live*.

1982 Appears in the movie *Doctor Detroit* starring Dan Aykroyd.

1984 Marries Adrienne Modell Rodriguez.

1985 Appears in *Rocky IV*, a movie starring Sylvester Stallone; "Living in America" reaches the *Billboard* Hot 100.

1986 Inducted into the Rock and Roll Hall of Fame in New York City; publishes his autobiography, *James Brown: The Godfather of Soul*.

1988 Sentenced to six years in prison following a series of felony charges for assault and possession of illegal drugs.

1992 Receives a Grammy for the Lifetime Achievement Award in New York City.

1997 Receives a star on the Hollywood Walk of Fame; featured during halftime of the Super Bowl.

2000 Inducted to the Songwriters Hall of Fame.

2001 Son, James Joseph Brown II, born.

2006 Dies on December 25, in Atlanta, Georgia, at Emory Crawford Long Hospital.

SOURCES

Chapter One: A Poor Boy From Georgia

p. 13,   "Because of all these . . ." James Brown, *James Brown the Godfather of Soul* (New York: Thunder's Mouth, 1997), 2.

p. 14,   "More than anything else . . ." Ibid., 266.

p. 14,   " No matter what came . . ." Ibid., 5.

p. 16,   "On the other side . . ." James Brown, *I Feel Good: A Memoir of a Life of Soul* (New York: New American Library, 2005), 67.

p. 16,   "Some people call it . . ." Brown, *The Godfather of Soul*, 16.

p. 17,   "I started dancing for nickels . . ." Nick Kent, "James Brown: Get Up, I Feel Like Being a Rap Machine," *NME*, September 15, 1979.

p. 19,   "I learned rhythm from the . . ." R. J. Smith, *The One: The Life and Music of James Brown* (New York: Gotham Books, 2012), 39.

p. 19,   "I'm sure a lot . . ." Brown, *The Godfather of Soul*, 18.

p. 24,   "I was nine . . ." Philip Norman, "James Brown: Mister Messiah," *Sunday Times*, 1971.

p. 25,   "If you don't allow . . ." Brown, *The Godfather of Soul*, 33.

Chapter Two: Please, Please, Please

p. 27,   "When Bobby went . . ." Barney Hoskyns, "James Brown: The Prisoner," *Mojo*, August 1998.

p. 29,   "When we saw . . ." Alan M. Leeds, Liner Notes for *Star Time*, James Brown, Polydor, 1991, 15.

p. 31,   "The Midnighters were the first . . ." Brown, *The Godfather of Soul*, 62.

p. 31,   "After that, I threw . . ." Brown, *I Feel Good*, 92.

p. 34,   "I didn't just want . . ." Ibid., 91.

p. 34,   "From then on . . ." "James Brown: Outasight," *Hullabaloo*, November 1966.

p. 38,   "I was working ten hours . . ." Michael Goldberg, "James Brown: Prisoner of Love Meets the Prisoners of Hate," *NME*, April 11, 1981.

Chapter Three: Live at the Apollo

p. 44,   "People who couldn't . . ." Brown, *The Godfather of Soul*, 129.

p. 45,   "the toughest audience . . ." Ibid., 86.

p. 47,   "group, led by James Brown . . ." "Apollo, N.Y.," *Variety*, December 16, 1959, in *The James Brown Reader: 50 Years of Writing About the Godfather of Soul*, ed. Nelson George and Alan Leeds (New York: Plume, 2008), 7.

p. 47,   "you ate there . . ." Brown, *The Godfather of Soul*, 99.

p. 50,   "which was every bit . . ." Brown, *I Feel Good*, 42.

SOURCES CONTINUED

p. 52,   "James was very intense . . ." Maycock, "The Making of James Brown *Live at the Apollo*."

p. 52,   "So now ladies and gentlemen . . ." "James Brown: The Original Hustler," Rappers.org, http://www.rappers.org/james-brown-the-original-hustler/.

p. 54,   "She brought the house . . ." Maycock, "The Making of James Brown *Live at the Apollo*."

Chapter Four: From Soul to Funk

p. 58,   "I guess I should get used . . ." "James Brown: Outasight,"*Hullabaloo*, November 1966.

p. 58,   "Within an hour . . ." Leeds, Liner Notes for *Star Time*, 9.

p. 59,   "Just when I should . . ." Brown, *The Godfather of Soul*, 150.

p. 60,   "It's a little beyond me . . ." Leeds, Liner Notes for *Star Time*, 9.

p. 60,   "James had wanted me . . ." Ibid.

p. 62,   "James called me in . . ." James Brown, Polydor, 1996, 3.

p. 66,   "I had just been through . . ." Brown, *The Godfather of Soul*, 147.

p. 67,   "While recording . . ." Brown, *I Feel Good*, 82–83.

pp. 68–69, "I had discovered . . ." Brown, *The Godfather of Soul*, 158.

pp. 68–69, "The 'One' is derived . . ." Smith, *The One: The Life and Music of James Brown*, 5.

p. 70,   "Right away, I got a new . . ." Leeds, Liner Notes for *Star Time*, 3.

Chapter Five: From Boston to Vietnam

p. 74,   "I clearly . . ." David Wiegand, "Godfather of Soul Changed Music at Frenetic Pace," (San Francisco) *Chronicle*, December 26, 2008.

p. 74,   "It was no longer . . ." Brown, *I Feel Good*, 132.

p. 75,   "If I can use . . ." Charlie Gillett, "James Brown: Telling the Natural Truth," *Record Mirror*, September 6, 1969.

p. 78,   "When a great man is killed . . ." Brown, *The Godfather of Soul*, 183.

p. 80,   "I'm here tonight . . ." Michael May, "The Godfather of Soul Saves Boston," Weekend America, April 5, 2008, http://weekendamerica. publicradio.org/.

p. 80,   "James Brown always gave his all," Ibid.

p. 81,   "Oreo Cookies," James Maycock, "Death or Glory: James Brown in Vietnam," *Mojo*, July 2003.

p. 81,   "I'd been trying . . ." Ibid.

p. 82,   "I went to perform . . ." Ibid.

p. 85,   "Flying into Saigon . . ." Ibid.

p. 86,   "The pilot said . . ." Ibid.

p. 87,   "The whole time . . ." Brown, *The Godfather of Soul*, 194.

Chapter Six: Tragedy, Taxes, and Disco
p. 90,   "I thought it was . . ." Brown, *The Godfather of Soul*, 202.
p. 91,   "They sent me a letter . . ." Barney Hoskyns, "Super Bad: James Brown,"
           Uncut, February 2004.
p. 92,   "He could sing and dance . . ." Brown, *I Feel Good*, 177.
p. 93,   "I became in effect his . . ." Philip Gourevitch, "Mr. Brown: On the
           Road With His Bad Self," *New Yorker*, July 29, 2002.
p. 94,   "I stand behind my regimen . . ." Hoskyns, "Super Bad: James Brown."
p. 94,   "I put in a system . . ." Brown, *The Godfather of Soul*, 112–113.
p. 96,   "So they watered down . . ." Kent, "James Brown: Get Up, I Feel Like
           Being a Rap Machine."
p. 99,   "I had a desire . . ." *Soul Power*, directed by Jeffrey Levy-Hinte (Sony,
           2008), DVD.
p. 99,   "I just feel . . ." Ibid.
p. 100,   "We touched the trees . . ." Jon Pareles, "Zaire's Moment of the Soul,"
           New York Times, July 5, 2009.
p. 100,   "His actions were suicidal . . ." Pat Kelly, "Papa Takes Some Mess,"
           Crawdaddy, December 1, 1975 in *The James Brown Reader: 50 Years of
           Writing About the Godfather of Soul*, ed. Nelson George and Alan Leeds
           (New York: Plume, 2008), 107.
p. 100,   "the best of James Brown . . ." *Soul Power*, directed by Jeffrey Levy-
           Hinte (Sony, 2008), DVD.

Chapter Seven: Home to Georgia
p. 109,   "His wife would call . . ." Pat Kelly, "James Brown: The Godfather's
           Back, with a Bullet," *Not Fade Away*, 1999 in *The James Brown Reader:
           50 Years of Writing About the Godfather of Soul*, ed. Nelson George and
           Alan Leeds (New York: Plume, 2008), 201.
pp. 109-11, "over the years . . ." Ibid., 200-201.
p. 111,   "He had grass . . ." Ibid., 199.
p. 112,   "Ironically, I landed . . ." Brown, *I Feel Good*, 208.
p. 112,   "PCP was such . . ." Hoskyns, "James Brown: The Prisoner."
p. 112,   " I wasn't arrested . . ." Brown, *I Feel Good*, 209–210.

BIBLIOGRAPHY

Brown, Geoff. *The Life of James Brown*. New York: Omnibus, 2008.

Brown, James. *James Brown: The Godfather of Soul*. New York: Thunder's Mouth, 1986.

————. *I Feel Good: A Memoir of a Life of Soul*. New York: Penguin, 2005.

George, Nelson. *The Death of Rhythm and Blues*. New York: Penguin, 1988.

————and Alan Leeds, eds. *The James Brown Reader: 50 Years of Writing About the Godfather of Soul*. New York: Plume, 2008.

Gourevitch, Philip. "Mr. Brown. On the Road With His Bad Self." *New Yorker*, July 29, 2002.

Guralnick, Peter. *Sweet Soul Music: Rhythm and Blues and the Dream of Southern Freedom*. New York: HarperCollins, 1986.

Hoskyns, Barney. "James Brown: The Prisoner." *Mojo*, August 1998.

Martin, Gavin. "James Brown (and Afrika Bambaataa): Sex Machine Today." *NME*, September 1984.

Maycock, James. "Death or Glory: James Brown in Vietnam." *Mojo*, July 2003.

————. "James Brown 1933–2006." *Independent*, December 26, 2006.

Norman, Philip. "James Brown: Mister Messiah." *Sunday Times*, 1971.

Rhodes, Don. *Say It Out Loud!: My Memories of Soul Brother No. 1*. Guilford, CT: Lyons, 2008.

Smith, R. J. *The One: The Life and Music of James Brown*. New York: Gotham Books, 2012.

Sullivan, James. *The Hardest Working Man: How James Brown Saved the Soul of America*. New York: Gotham, 2008.

Vincent, Ricky. *Funk: The Music, the People, and the Rhythm of the One*. New York: St. Martin's Griffin, 1995.

Wesley, Fred. *Hit Me, Fred: Recollections of a Sideman*. Durham, NC: Duke University, 2002.

Witter, Simon. "James Brown." *Sky*, 1990.

Wolk, Douglas. *James Brown's Live at the Apollo*. New York: Continuum, 2004.

WEB SITES

http://www.allmusic.com/

Allmusic Guide includes a short biography of James Brown, an extensive discography, and reviews of many of his albums.

http://www.bmi.com/

James Brown received a BMI (Broadcast Music Inc.) Icon Award in 2002, and the Web site includes footage of Brown accepting the award along with other videos of the singer.

http://www.kennedy-center.org/explorer/

The Kennedy Center honored Brown in 2003 and the Center's Web site includes a biography of Brown.

http://www.rockhall.com

The Web site for the Rock and Roll Hall of Fame and museum includes information on inductees and exhibitions.

http://www.rollingstone.com/

The *Rolling Stone* Web site is operated by *Rolling Stone* magazine, and includes a number of archived articles focusing on James Brown.

http://songwritershalloffame.org/

The Songwriters Hall of Fame has a separate page for Brown that includes a biography, song catalogue, and a list of recommended materials.

INDEX

PHOTO CREDITS

All images used in this book that are not in the public domain are credited in the listing that follows:

Cover: Pictorial Press Ltd/Alamy
2: Time & Life Pictures/Getty Images
4-5: Redferns
8: Pictorial Press Ltd/Alamy
10: Timothy A. Clary/AFP/
    Getty Images/Newscom
13: Courtesy of Library of Congress
14: Courtesy of Library of Congress
15: Courtesy of Library of Congress
17: Courtesy of Library of Congress
19: Courtesy of Scurlock Studio Records,
    Archives Center, National Museum of
    American History
20: Courtesy of Library of Congress
21: Courtesy of Library of Congress
22-23: Courtesy of Library of Congress
24: Courtesy of Library of Congress
25: Courtesy of Library of Congress
26: Getty Images
28: Courtesy of Library of Congress
30: Pictorial Press Ltd/Alamy
35: Granamour Weems Collection/Alamy
36-37: Associated Press
40: Michael Ochs Archives/Getty Images
42-43: Michael Ochs Archives/Getty Images
45: Courtesy William P. Gottlieb Collection/
    Library of Congress
46: Courtesy William P. Gottlieb Collection/
    Library of Congress
48-49: Everett Collection Historical/Alamy
51: Courtesy of Library of Congress
52-53: Michael Ochs Archives/Getty Images
56: Pictorial Press Ltd/Alamy
61: Michael Ochs Archives/Getty Images
62-63: Associated Press
64-65: Courtesy of Library of Congress
68-69: Michael Ochs Archives/Getty Images
72: Flip Schulke/Corbis
74-75: Courtesy of Library of Congress
77: Courtesy of Library of Congress
78: Courtesy of Library of Congress
82-83: Christian Simonpietri/Sygma/Corbis
84: Bettmann/Corbis/AP Images
86-87: Courtesy of U.S. Army
88: Associated Press
90: Bettmann/Corbis/AP Images

93: Associated Press
96-97: Courtesy CC-BY-SA
98-99: Photos 12/Alamy
102: David P. Gilkey/ZUMA press/Newscom
104-105: Photos 12/Alamy
107: Photos 12/Alamy
110: Associated Press
113: Mug Shot/Alamy
114-115: Associated Press
116: Newscom (Bruno Mars)
116-117: Getty Images (w/ Will.i.am
    & Timberlake)
117: Associated Press (w/ Michael Jackson),
    Newscom (w/ Usher)